FORTRESS • 86

ENGLISH CASTLES
1200–1300

CHRISTOPHER GRAVETT   ILLUSTRATED BY ADAM HOOK

Series editors Marcus Cowper and Nikolai Bogdanovic

First published in 2009 by Osprey Publishing
Midland House, West Way, Botley, Oxford OX2 0PH, UK
443 Park Avenue South, New York, NY 10016, USA
E-mail: info@ospreypublishing.com

ISBN 978 1 84603 374 2
E-book ISBN 978 1 84908 083 5

Editorial by Ilios Publishing Ltd, Oxford UK (www.iliospublishing.com)
Cartography: Map Studio, Romsey, UK
Front cover image: © iStockphoto.com/KarlDolenc
Page layout by Ken Vail Graphic Design, Cambridge, UK (kvgd.com)
Index by Auriol Griffith-Jones
Originated by PPS Grasmere Ltd
Printed in China through Bookbuilders

09 10 11 12 13   10 9 8 7 6 5 4 3 2 1

A CIP catalogue record for this book is available from the British Library.

DEDICATION

In memory of my mother and father.

EDITOR'S NOTE

Unless otherwise indicated, all the images in this volume are the property of the author.

ARTIST'S NOTE

Readers may care to note that the original paintings from which the colour plates in this book were prepared are available for private sale. All reproduction copyright whatsoever is retained by the Publishers. All enquiries should be addressed to:

Scorpio Gallery, PO Box 475, Hailsham, East Sussex, BN27 2SL, UK

The Publishers regret that they can enter into no correspondence upon this matter.

THE FORTRESS STUDY GROUP (FSG)

The object of the FSG is to advance the education of the public in the study of all aspects of fortifications and their armaments, especially works constructed to mount or resist artillery. The FSG holds an annual conference in September over a long weekend with visits and evening lectures, an annual tour abroad lasting about eight days, and an annual Members' Day.

The FSG journal FORT is published annually, and its newsletter Casemate is published three times a year. Membership is international. For further details, please contact:

The Secretary, c/o 6 Lanark Place, London W9 1BS, UK

Website: www.fsgfort.com

THE WOODLAND TRUST

Osprey Publishing are supporting the Woodland Trust, the UK's leading woodland conservation charity, by funding the dedication of trees.

FOR A CATALOGUE OF ALL BOOKS PUBLISHED BY OSPREY MILITARY AND AVIATION PLEASE CONTACT:

Osprey Direct, c/o Random House Distribution Center, 400 Hahn Road, Westminster, MD 21157
Email: uscustomerservice@ospreypublishing.com

Osprey Direct, The Book Service Ltd, Distribution Centre, Colchester Road, Frating Green, Colchester, Essex, CO7 7DW
E-mail: customerservice@ospreypublishing.com

www.ospreypublishing.com

CONTENTS

ENGLISH CASTLES 1200–1300

INTRODUCTION

In the 150 years since the Norman Conquest, England had become a more unified nation. The 13th century would see conflict not between the conquerors and the conquered but between the king and factions of his own baronage. In the two civil wars that dogged England, rebel factions tried to control the king but there were always magnates and lesser men who stood by their monarch. Only in the border regions of Wales and Scotland did English kings come up against other sovereign states.

The king at the turn of the 13th century was John, an Angevin with Norman blood. Though in some ways a better ruler than his selfish brother and predecessor, Richard the Lionheart, John alienated a section of the baronage. The controls imposed by his father, Henry II, John's own character, the loss of Normandy to France in 1204 and failure to regain it brought matters to a head at Runnymede in 1215, where baronial demands were set down in the Magna Carta, which solved little. Civil war still broke out and the rebels invited Prince Louis, son of Phillip II of France, to take the English throne. There was a possibility that Alexander II might descend from Scotland and the Welsh princes caused problems along the marches. John had been busy

At Barnard Castle a large single-aisled timber hall was replaced in the early 13th century by a new stone building some 13.4 × 8.95m (44 × 29.4ft). The lord's chamber and the donjon were at one end (right) so the common door into the hall seems to have been placed at its opposite end.

recruiting troops from Poitou and Flemish mercenaries and strengthening many royal castles throughout England, whose garrisons threatened rebel lands and hampered their owners from using soldiers elsewhere. Following John's death in 1216, many magnates continued to resist Louis who eventually withdrew. The war had been one of sieges with both sides reluctant to commit to the luck of pitched battle.

John's son, now Henry III, was aged nine and so until 1227 was under the tutelage of Hubert de Burgh and his rival, Peter des Roches. The war had allowed the Welsh Prince, Llywelyn the Great, to seize nearly all of Wales and in 1218 the Treaty of Worcester granted him royal castles at Carmarthen and Cardigan and the wardship of the heir of southern Powys. When the great William Marshal died in 1219 Llywelyn attacked the honour of Pembroke, only to see the earl's son cross from Ireland to capture Carmarthen and Cardigan and secure the valley of the Tywi and northern Dyfed respectively. Royal power needed establishing in vital areas; Builth could watch Snowdonia and the Wye Valley, while Montgomery could galvanize the eastern Marches and block access to Shrewsbury.

Llywelyn died in 1240 and his son, David, came to London and did homage for north Wales but failure to come to arbitration gave Henry III the excuse to invade and overrun north Wales up to David's castle of Deganwy (Gannoc) near the river Conwy. Henry involved himself with Gruffydd, David's brother and captive, but following negotiations Gruffydd was taken instead to comfortable captivity in the Tower of London and died in 1244 trying to escape using knotted sheets. David soon revolted and Henry gathered an army, including troops from Ireland. Henry had to withdraw and David died in February 1246. Gruffydd's sons, Llywelyn and Owain, continued to resist but then made peace and in 1247 surrendered the lands between Chester and the Conwy Valley. Eventually Llywelyn took control and assumed the title 'prince of Wales' in 1258. He made attacks on Builth and the marcher lands until recognized by the Treaty of Montgomery in 1267.

In England Henry, a lover of the arts and perhaps most famous for rebuilding Westminster Abbey, faced the rising star of Simon de Montfort, earl of Leicester, and son of a ruthless French crusader; he had married Henry's

The walls, outer gate and remains of the barbican at William Marshal's powerful castle at Pembroke, dating largely from about 1200.

English Castles 1100–1300

SCOTLAND

NORTH SEA

IRELAND

Bamburgh

Newcastle-upon-Tyne

IRISH SEA

Brougham
Brough
Barnard Castle

Middleham
Pickering

Clifford's Tower

Sandal
Pontefract

Peveril

Beeston

Lincoln
Bolingbroke

Montgomery
Castell Bryn Amlwg
Acton Burnell
ENGLAND

Hopton
Stokesay
Ludlow

WALES
Kenilworth
Rockingham
Barnwell

Grosmont
Bedford

Kidwelly
Skenfrith

Pembroke
Tretower
Goodrich

Manorbier
White Castle

St Briavels
Chepstow
Oxford
Berkhamsted

Caerphilly

Tower of London

Windsor
Hadleigh

Rochester

Winchester
Allington

Tiverton
Tonbridge
Dover

Tintagel
Okehampton
Arundel

Launceston
Pevensey

Restormel
Corfe

ENGLISH CHANNEL

N

| 0 | | 50 miles |
| 0 | | 100km |

sister and been given Kenilworth Castle as a residence. However, Simon became involved in baronial discontent that led to the Provisions of Oxford in 1258, which formed the basis for the first parliaments in England. The Lord Edward (the future Edward I) seemed to be siding increasingly with Simon and, while Henry was in France, Llywelyn attacked south and then north Wales, seizing castles until the Treaty of Montgomery called a halt to hostilities.

Meanwhile Simon returned and, having attracted a rebel element around him, instigated a civil war known as the Barons' War. Henry was not militarily skilled but his brother, Richard, and son, the Lord Edward, organized the opposition. Although Henry and Edward were captured after the battle of Lewes in 1264, Simon's triumph was brief. Despite gaining authority in the west by the Pact of Worcester with the Marcher lords in 1264 his star was waning and, following Edward's escape in May 1265, Simon was butchered at the battle of Evesham. Lingering resistance was finally smothered and the rest of Henry's reign was relatively peaceful.

After Henry died in 1272, Edward took the throne. Somewhat violent and unpredictable, he was destined to become one of the most formidable of English kings. Relatively secure on his throne he turned his attention first to Wales in 1277, where Llywelyn had stirred up revolt the previous year. In three invasions he effectively crushed all opposition by 1295, building a chain of massive castles to contain any revolts. Already he was looking towards Scotland, where he supported a puppet king in John Balliol. When a faction of the Scots rebelled under William Wallace and routed an English army at Stirling Bridge in 1297, Edward marched north and defeated the Scottish pike formations at Falkirk the following year. Wallace was captured and executed and although Scotland was quiet the borders would remain uncertain for centuries. As a separate kingdom, Scotland's castles do not form part of this book but English-built castles in the principality of Wales will be covered. The great Edwardian fortifications in Wales are the subject of a separate volume.

The domestic block at Grosmont (c.1201–04) had an undercroft, unequally divided into two, with a first-floor hall (with fireplace) and solar, originally reached via an external timber stair. It is likely to be Hubert de Burgh's work, perhaps inspired by his hall at Christchurch Castle. However, when he replaced the timber palisades in stone (c.1220s) two new doorways (centre) were punched through at ground level, the first-floor division was removed and a central dividing wall added. This was perhaps to alter the hall block into a service block (with a well and fireplace in the south-eastern ground floor room that may indicate a kitchen) to serve a new wooden hall butted against its long side.

CHRONOLOGY

1199		Death of Richard I, accession of John.
1204		Loss of Normandy.
1214		Battle of Bouvines, defeat of Anglo-Imperial army by Phillip II of France.
1215	May	Siege of Northampton castle by rebels.
	15 June	Magna Carta. Civil war breaks out.
	October–December	Siege of Rochester Castle by John.
	December 1215 to March 1216	Harrying expedition through England by John. Surrender of Rockingham, Belvoir, Pontefract, York, Richmond, Durham, Warkworth, Alnwick, Berwick, Skelton, Fotheringay, Bedford, Framlingham, Colchester, Hedingham and Hertford.
1216	May	Prince Louis of France invades England on invitation of rebels.
	May–July	Surrender to Louis of Reigate, Guildford, Farnham, Winchester, Odiham, Marlborough and Worcester.
	July–October	Siege of Dover castle by Prince Louis.
	September	John enters Lincoln.
	October	Death of John, accession of Henry III under tutors Hubert de Burgh and Peter des Roches. Truce agreed at Dover.
	November 1216 to January 1217	Surrender to Louis of Hertford, Berkhamsted, Colchester, Orford, Norwich, Cambridge, Pleshey and Hedingham.
1217	February	Louis returns to France.
	April	Louis comes back to England.
	May	Louis resumes siege of Dover. Siege and battle of Lincoln by William Marshal. Siege of Dover raised.
	August	Sea battle off Sandwich, rebels defeated.
	September	Louis agrees terms and leaves England.
1218		Treaty of Worcester gives Llywelyn Carmarthen and Cardigan castles.
1219		Death of William Marshal, Llywelyn attacks Pembroke.
1220		Henry III comes of age. Hubert de Burgh demands rebel strongholds be given up. Capture of Rockingham Castle.
1223		Hubert de Burgh leads army to relieve Builth.
1224		Siege of Bedford Castle by Henry III.
1231		Revolt of Llywelyn. Campaign of Elfiel by Hubert de Burgh and latter's fall from power.

1240		Death of Llywelyn the Great.
1241		Cardigan and Builth retaken by the English.
1244		Death of Gruffydd, son of Llywelyn the Great.
1245		Henry invades Wales; rebuilds Deganwy.
1246		Death of David, son of Llywelyn the Great.
1247		Peace of Woodstock between Henry and Welsh princes Llywelyn, son of Gruffydd, and his brother Owain.
1255		Llywelyn in civil war of Owain.
1256		Llywelyn attacks the four Cantrefs.
1257		Richard of Cornwall elected king of the Romans.
1258		The Provisions of Oxford. Llywelyn assumes title 'prince of Wales'
1262		Llywelyn attacks Mortimer and overruns Brecon.
1263		Llywelyn attacks Abergavenny, destroys Dyserth Castle and recovers Deganwy.
1264	February	Henry of Montfort tricks himself into Gloucester town. Robert de Ferrers storms Worcester.
	April	Edward seizes Northampton town and then the castle. Partial capture of Rochester Castle by Simon de Montfort and recapture by Henry III.
	May	Battle of Lewes: capture of Henry III and Prince Edward by Simon de Montfort.
1265		Battle of Evesham: death of Simon de Montfort.
1266		Siege of Kenilworth Castle by Henry III.
1267		Treaty of Montgomery: Henry III acknowledges Llywelyn ap Gruffydd as prince of Wales.
1272		Death of Henry III, accession of Edward I.
1276		Llywelyn refuses homage to Edward I.
1277		First Welsh War against Llywelyn ap Gruffydd.
1282		Second Welsh War against Llywelyn ap Gruffydd. Death of Llywelyn.
1283		End of Second Welsh War. Dafydd captured and executed.
1284		Prince Edward (future Edward II) born at Caernarfon. Statute of Rhuddlan creates new counties of Anglesey, Caernarfon, Merioneth, Cardigan and Carmarthen, with Caernarfon as the centre.
1287		Revolt of David.
1293–94		Third Welsh War against Madog ap Llywelyn.

1297	Edward invades Scotland. Battle of Stirling Bridge and defeat of English by William Wallace.
1298	Battle of Falkirk and defeat of Scots by Edward I.
1301	Prince Edward created prince of Wales. Capture and execution of William Wallace.
1307	Death of Edward I. Accession of Edward II.

DESIGN AND DEVELOPMENT

At the beginning of the 13th century a few castles remained simple enclosures bounded by ditch and palisade, perhaps with a timber gate tower and some wall towers. The motte and bailey added a mound topped by palisades and a timber tower. Even in 1204 King John was repairing his wooden castles in Shropshire. Stone walls and mural towers were not completed at Corfe until about 1285; until then some parts were still of timber. The replacement of palisades on a motte with stone walls created a 'shell keep', within whose protective walls buildings were set around (such as Windsor and Arundel). At Restormel in Cornwall a shell keep sits on natural high ground in the middle of a ring work. However, the great tower, or donjon (from the 16th century also called a 'keep'), was still the dominating feature of many castles. Their numbers had multiplied during the 12th century and in the later years of the century cylindrical versions began to appear but were mostly seen in the West Country and in Norman castles built in Wales. Some donjons that appear to sit on a motte actually have their foundations on solid ground, with the earth piled around the walls to protect the base of the tower. However, some were placed on top, with the weight of stone on a man-made mound risking subsidence. A classic instance of this is Clifford's Tower in York; floods in 1315–16 weakened the base of the artificial mound and caused subsidence, which had caused the tower to crack in two places by 1360, as seen today.

It has been suggested that the introduction of stronger curtain walls and flanking towers heralded the demise of the donjon. Lacking true arrow loops

Hubert's curtain walls with D-shaped mural towers and a gate tower at Grosmont were constructed between 1219 and 1232, being built up against the earlier hall block rather than enclosing it.

and largely limited to passive defence, these structures may have seemed white elephants. However, many donjons appear to have been built as much as statements of lordship, for entertaining or as private suites and these functions continued throughout the period, sometimes assisted by upgrading architectural details such as windows, as was done by the sons of William Marshal in the 11th-century donjon at Chepstow. Their basements also remained useful storage areas. Existing donjons could be amalgamated within new work as functional buildings – an example being the White Tower, the huge early donjon at the Tower of London. This continuity of function would develop into the tower house of the 14th and 15th centuries. It cannot be denied that fewer new donjons were erected in the 13th century but they still appeared. The quadrilobe design of Clifford's Tower was copied from Etampes in France. At Pontefract a lobed donjon was erected by

The early 13th-century castle at Skenfrith, Gwent, has a cylindrical donjon within a curtain with D-shaped towers like those at contemporary Grosmont. Together with White Castle these form the 'Three Castles' built by Hubert de Burgh in the area. The foundations of a contemporary range of three rooms lie close by.

the Lacys and brought up to date in the 14th century by John of Gaunt. The great cylindrical tower at Barnard Castle was erected in about 1200, while Edward I was building a similar shape on the old motte at Cambridge in 1288 and he seems to have favoured a shell keep at Builth, as did his father at Pickering. Edward erected another cylindrical but otherwise unique design in about 1270 at Flint in Wales.

A huge number of castles were already established across Britain by 1200 and this number actually reduced as the Angevin kings took tighter control of unauthorized castle building. Therefore most of the building work carried out during the next century, especially in England, was not on new structures but on improving the lot of existing castles. Some new castles were built, such as Bolingbroke (Lincolnshire) and Beeston (Cheshire). These examples were essentially fortified enceintes, curtain walls set with mural towers and lacking a donjon, on similar lines to the earlier layout at Framlingham. What had changed by the 13th century was the strength of defence afforded to the perimeter. Higher, sturdier walls with cylindrical or D-shaped flanking towers – or in the case of Dyserth, polygonal – set more regularly and in greater number, contrasted with many earlier defences that had often been of wood.

Some castles, such as Chepstow, had more than one bailey but were similar to Richard I's stronghold of Château Gaillard in Normandy, in that an enemy was expected to fight his way through one defended area after another, sometimes with a donjon (usually already existing) as a final defence. However, here strength relied more on providing several obstacles, without necessarily having the benefit of supporting fire from all walls. The early use of concentric defences seen in the 12th-century work at Dover continued but such layouts never achieved such popularity as might be expected. This design of two lines of wall mutually supporting one another has been described as the high peak of castle design. However, it was by its very nature extremely

Towers

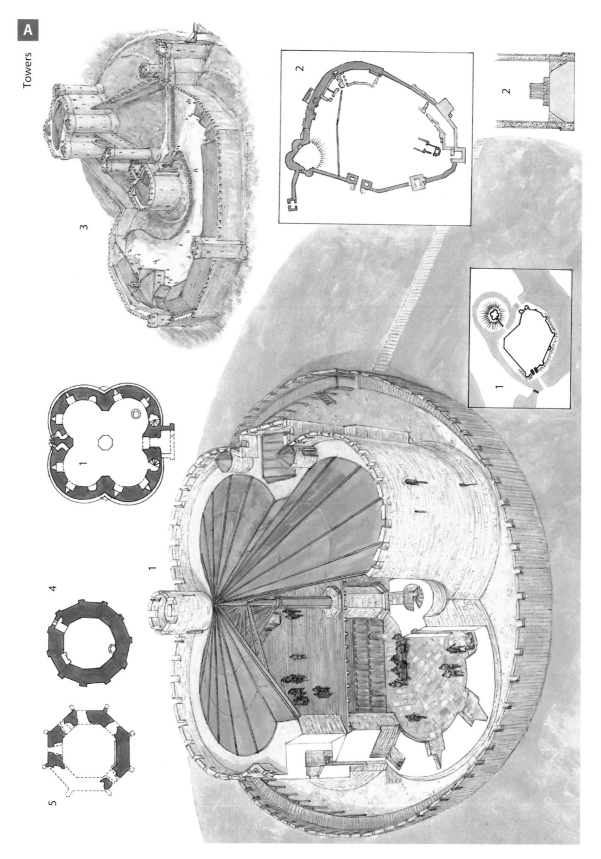

The Bailey Gate led from the town into the fortifications at Castle Acre in the early 13th century.

expensive owing to the amount of stone required. After Dover, very few castles in England would become concentric, although excavations at Banbury suggest concentric walls that may date to about 1230. However, the English-built Caerphilly, Denbigh, Harlech and Beaumaris in Wales (the latter pair the work of Edward I himself) are all concentric. As a compromise to the massive costs involved in concentric defence, a number of castles were adapted so that only the weakest side or sides were provided with an extra line of defence. This meant that where rock outcrops or cliff faces etc were utilized, a double line of walls would only be used on the weakest sides, the probable direction from which an attack would come. The first stone building period of *c*.1275 at Kidwelly saw a straightforward quadrilateral layout with the four angles covered by large circular towers standing within a 12th-century semicircular ditch whose palisade was upgraded to stone in the early 14th century, while the fourth (eastern) side was protected by the sharp drop to the river Gwendraeth below.

However, as is evident from the castle building carried out by Edward I, there is no convenient direct line of development that can be used to illustrate a progression in castle design. One of the foremost castle builders of the time, Edward used a variety of designs as seen in his Welsh fortresses: donjons that were almost motte and bailey in design (Flint), fortified enceintes (Conwy and Caernarfon) and concentric (Harlech, Beaumaris).

A TOWERS

Clifford's Tower (1) was a quadrilobe building with a palisade round the summit of the motte. A central pillar supported the beams for the first floor with the royal apartments, where there was a chapel. Water from the river Foss was diverted into an artificial lake, the King's Pool.

Pontefract (2) had an irregular lobed tower, built up around an earlier motte, the widening internal gap being filled in.

A strong tower was built on the motte at Sandal (3). The large barbican tower with ashlar facings had a guardroom with latrine and presumably rooms on the now-lost level above. Entrance from the bailey was over a bridge (footings remain); a pit 3.8m (12.5ft) long and over three metres (ten feet) deep formed the inner side of a turning bridge, with possible other defences. A right turn led to a door barring the bridge (again, footings remain) across the motte ditch up to the gate. This and rather weak bailey walls and gate suggest the garrison intended to concentrate on the inner castle.

Plans of the polygonal donjon at Tickhill (4) built by Henry II, *c*.1178-80 and Odiham (5) built by King John, *c*.1207-12.

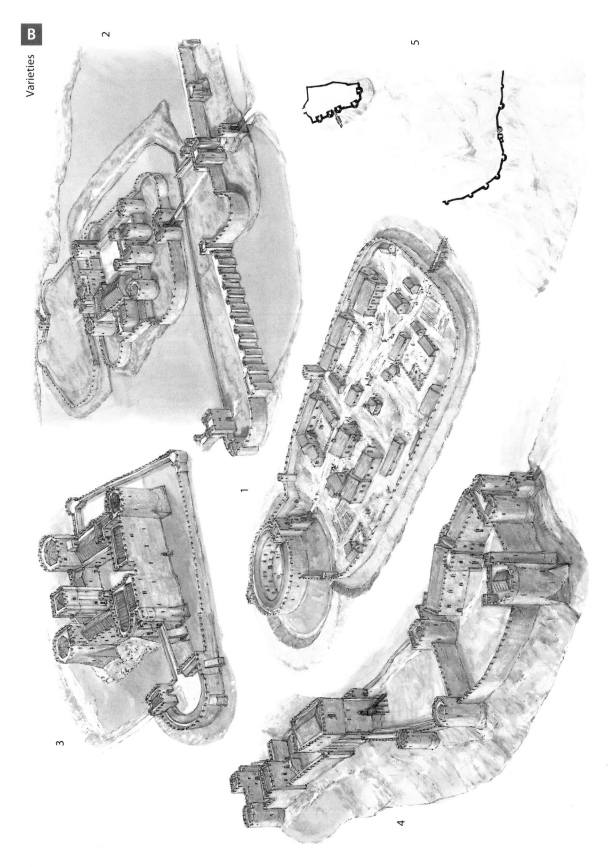

The most impressive advance in fortification was in the design of the gatehouse. Already at the beginning of the century some powerful examples were being constructed with twin towers either side of the gate passage as opposed to a single tower or none at all. By the end of the century some of the most powerful gates in Europe had been built, set with multiple defences and suites of domestic quarters above. The entrance to a castle, that most vulnerable area, had become its strongest part. As gates were strengthened, their outer side was sometimes provided with an additional fortification, the barbican.

By 1300 the castle had effectively reached its apogee. It was as secure as could be designed within the limits of its owner's purse, with every defensive trick available if required. The king effectively held the majority of powerful royal castles and under that most formidable monarch, Edward I, money had been poured into his fortresses to provide the equal of anything seen in Europe.

Town defences

Many towns had grown up with the planting of Norman castles. New or rebuilt castles in potentially turbulent areas might spawn a town beside them, and these were actively encouraged by Edward I in Wales, and there are also many town walls in the north of England. Often these town walls were status symbols rather than military fortifications. These defences tended to appear in the 13th century (or even later), being financed by a murage grant that allowed taxes to be raised or tolls levied, although not all building was thus assisted

Hubert de Burgh blocked solid the Norfolk Towers, damaged after the 1216 siege of Dover, and added the cylindrical St John's Tower (far left) in the ditch, reached via a passage, to flay the area with missiles.

B   VARIETIES

The late-13th-century shell keep at Restormel sits on a low natural motte, the bailey also protected by a curtain wall (1).

Caerphilly not only has massive water defences but was also a powerful concentric castle (2), completed c.1290. A spit of gravel between two streams was cut off to create an island for the castle, connected to a smaller island (the West Platform), while the North Bank (made from earth from the ditches) created the outer bank of a moat as well. The North and South lakes were controlled by strongly defended dams to prevent the lakes being drained. Gilbert de Clare, present at the siege of Kenilworth, may have been inspired by those effective defences to construct his own version at Caerphilly.

Built in the late 13th century, Goodrich had stout rock ditches on the south and west sides but an outer wall was added on the two other sides to increase the fortification, making the castle partially concentric (3).

Chepstow is sited along a cliff top overlooking the river Wye (4). The 11th-century donjon effectively cuts off the Upper Bailey and its barbican from the Middle and Lower baileys. Much of the castle is of various periods in the late 12th and 13th centuries, with Roger Bigod's work (c.1270-1306) seen in the domestic range and huge mural tower in the Lower Bailey (foreground).

(5) Largely dating from c.1220–1240, Beeston's surviving section of outer curtain shows how it girdled the lower slopes of a crag, the inner ward crowning the summit beyond.

and, conversely, some grants were not used to build walls. Royal boroughs were usually given walls. For strategic or financial reasons walls might slice through existing street layouts. If a castle was present the walls usually met those of the castle (as at Ludlow). Sometimes stone replaced the timber palisades of previous centuries. Some towns that could not afford complete walls made do with gates across main roads, which also assisted in the charging of tolls.

At Launceston in Cornwall the walls and gates were built towards the end of the 13th century (the Eastgate and some wall sections survive). Some gatehouses had a chapel as in castle construction. Nearly all the new towns in Wales were given defences and some of the best walls of the period are those at Conwy and Caernarfon, described in another volume. The walls at Newcastle-upon-Tyne, dating from the second half of the 13th century, provide a useful insight into town fortification. In places they are six metres (20ft) high and two metres (seven feet) thick, with the parados overhanging the rear face of the wall and supported by corbels. Most towers are D-shaped and set at fairly regular intervals with a ditch dug in front after the walls were built. Each consists of a single vaulted storey, lit by loops and accessed from the rear at ground level. The battlement level that rose above the walls either side was accessed via steps from the wall walk. Each tower was provided with a permanent set of corbels, to carry wooden hoardings to overlook the wall base. In order to supplement these towers there are in addition turrets that sit upon the wall at intervals but project backwards on corbels. Each is furnished with a single loop and gave some protection from the elements to sentries entering via the wall-walk. The battlement level of the turret was reached by an external stair. Together with these defences were several gates, each consisting of a passage flanked by twin towers, the West Gate with a barbican and also water gates and sally ports.

Building castles

Royal castle work was largely under the control of the local sheriff, who looked after the finances involved, while 'viewers', non-technical inspectors, checked progress and actively itinerant kings like John saw at first hand what was being done. Towards the end of the 12th century the financial side was passed usually to the constable of a castle when major work was to be done, and by about 1210 supervision was being given to a man designated for a particular site operation. The name *custodes operacionum* – 'keepers of the works' – began to be applied to such men, who became more established under Henry III.

The 12th-century outer curtain at Dover was reinforced by King John and Henry III. The former built Crèvecoeur Tower (far left) and Godsfoe Tower, whose square design may be attributable to it being the chamber block to a hall. Henry built the Constable's Gateway (far right) with flanking towers.

Ingeniatores (or engineers) under King John include Fortinus, who received a robe in 1203–04 for work repairing Colchester Castle, and William Baiard at Nottingham (1204–05). Master Urri was mainly hired to oversee the royal siege engines, including those in France and Ireland. Master Albert was rewarded by John for his services, while Master Elyas of Oxford, who first appears on the Pipe Roll in 1187, worked for John on Oxford, Portchester and the Tower before disappearing in 1203. *Ingeniatores* in the records of the 12th and early 13th centuries may have been responsible for buildings or for siege engines (and on campaign) and do not seem to have as defined a role as the small band of master craftsmen employed such as Master Osbert, a mason (*petrarius*) at Gloucester Castle in 1207 and later Corfe. Both select groups were paid from the royal Wardrobe. King John had more carpenters working during his reign than other types, mainly because of the requirements of siege warfare. Master Nicholas de Andeli was a French carpenter (who possibly worked on Château Gaillard in Normandy) in service about 40 years under John and Henry III, dying in 1245; William the Englishman was a master (died 1214) as was Richard de Arches (at Oxford Castle in 1215).

Henry III had 58 royal castles directly under his control when he came of age in 1227 but grants saw this increasingly fall to 47 at the time of his death. He had several master craftsmen including some noted above: Master Stephen (master mason at Corfe in 1213 and the new hall at Winchester); Master Simon of Northampton (carpenter, mentioned from 1226 – worked at Windsor and at York in 1245); and Master Henry de Rayns (given robe as master of king's masons in 1243 – York in 1245). Special inquests highlighted misconduct by sheriffs in using funds for building, as for example at Nottingham Castle in 1255, and the king decided to act. He named Master John of Gloucester (mason) and Master Alexander the carpenter 'chief masters of all works of castles, manors and houses on this side of Trent and Humber' in 1257, and they were kept busy, as at Portchester Castle in 1256, viewing defects. When both had died, Robert of Beverley was appointed 'chief viewer' of the Tower, Windsor, Rochester and Hadleigh castles in 1271.

Under Edward I the most famous master was James of St George, a Savoyard who was the genius behind many of the king's greatest works in Wales. In the late 13th century Philip Scrope is recorded as a local mason working at Corfe, while Master Thomas of Houghton was a carpenter serving the king in England, Wales and Scotland. A carpenter called Robert of Colebrook was working especially at the Tower.

Master Peter was employed by Roger Leyburn to strengthen the hoardings at Sandwich and to organize the making of stone shot for the catapults; these were carefully shaped into spheres of a required size by masons, not simply used as they came out of the ground; standardizing size and weight assisted in making each shot fall within a similar target area.

Castle planning was a matter of consultation between the king or lord and his master mason. New castles might take account of natural defensive features, such as cliffs, while rock foundations deterred mining and rivers were good for access and controlling traffic. Once the site was agreed the defensive ditches or moats could be dug by the ditch diggers (*fossatores*) and miners (*minatores*), who also worked on vaults and foundations. Ditches were the first obstacle to any attack and a boon when working in unsettled areas such as the marches of Wales or Scotland. A natural source of such labour was the fenlands of eastern England, together with Norfolk and Suffolk, although Yorkshire, Cheshire and Northamptonshire also sent high numbers. If a river needed diverting or was to be utilized in flooding a moat then experienced workers were needed to achieve this using dams or sluices.

In potentially hostile areas timber palisades might be erected first to shield the men working on the stone walls. However, at Restormel the gatehouse seems to have been built first, to protect the weakest spot before the main walls were begun, while in 1204 John ordered the justiciar of Ireland to build the tower at Dublin castle first, followed by 'a castle and bailey', so that the strongest point was established. Walls were built up often in levels with work carrying on until the weather deteriorated, when the stone would be covered by straw or thatch to protect it from frost until spring. Sometimes it is possible to trace each year's building period in a given wall.

Different types of mason were used: hewers or quarriers (*quareatores*) freed the stone from the quarry, using wedges to split the rock; rough masons (*petrarii*) then cut the blocks. Expensive, dressed ashlar stone was often limited to corners, door, window or loop surrounds, or battlements; for this, free masons were employed, who also carved capitals and decorated the window apertures in the finer rooms with tracery. Frequently walls were built as two skins, between which was a mass of rock and stone bonded with mortar and sometimes strengthened by rods or chains set across the wall to help bind everything together. Local stone was often utilized; shillet was used at Restormel in Cornwall, with only small areas of good white stone, probably brought 16km (ten miles) from Pentewan. Red sandstone was used at many castles such as Goodrich. Magnesium limestone was used at Clifford's Tower. Mortar was made from quicklime, the stone being heated in a furnace to break it up before being mixed with water on site by lime burners.

Sometimes the original layout was altered following partial erection, as seems to have happened at Grosmont and White Castle (and possibly at Caerphilly), where the axis of the castles was turned through 90 degrees in the 1260s. Not all work was on new building or the replacement of timber by stone. Corfe had work carried out on the donjon a number of times, especially when King John was building his residential suite, the 'Gloriette',

The great hall at Winchester has the largest internal areas of any 13th-century hall, with twin rows of aisle pillars. On the wall hangs the 'Round Table', a 13th-century construction repainted in the 16th century and probably used in the pageants known as 'Round Tables'.

next to it. In 1244 the exterior was roughcast to deal with masonry defects and then whitened. The donjon was heightened in 1293–94, overseen by Brother Bernard who seems to have been a carpenter. Towers were sometimes given names: at Corfe in the 1280s, work was completed on four towers called 'Butavant', 'Cockayne', 'Plenty' and 'Sauveray'.

Carpenters were required in great numbers, initially to provide the scaffolding, which was of two kinds, either placed against the walls or on horizontal beams supported in holes left in the wall face called putlogs. The diagonal or spiral setting of such holes on some buildings came from Savoy and allowed stones to be dragged up the sloping planked trackway, rather than cranes having to be used, which slowed progress; human treadmills could turn larger examples. By this method stones could be hoisted using pincers that utilized leverage to grip securely; winches were used to haul buckets. Carpenters also fashioned roof timbers and trusses, ceiling beams and floorboards, the former set into holes in the wall or else supported on stone corbels. The great gatehouse doors and moveable bridge had to be constructed with perhaps a timber bridge partly spanning the ditch. Doors and window shutters, drawbars, ladders, cupboards or wall cupboard doors, bed frames, tables, benches and a few chairs and footstools were needed. Defensive siege engines might also be required. Buildings in the bailey might be of timber and timber framing was commonly employed instead of planking or posts, the spaces filled with wattle and daub – a mixture of straw, mud and manure – that was then whitewashed. The north tower at the fortified manor of Stokesay has clay blockwork between the timbers of its projecting first-floor walls. Lead, tiles, wooden shingles or thatch could be used for roofing. *Hurdatores* made the hoardings, the timber galleries erected along battlements.

Set squares, dividers and compasses, plumb lines and other instruments were basically similar to those of today. Metal tools would become blunt or break, so smiths were needed to sharpen or repair them constantly, as well as to produce hinges, latches, chains and the thousands of iron nails to hold things together. Coal was brought to the site for their furnaces and for the mortar fires. In 1275 Master Henry of Lewes entered service as the king's smith at the Tower of London, specifically creating military articles. Plasterers decorated room interiors. Master William, the king's painter who supervised work at Windsor for Henry III, was a monk of Westminster. Carters and packhorses were a necessity to convey materials and this cost huge sums. Food and drink had to be provided, and in unsettled territory an armed guard provided.

John spent more on castles than any other of the Angevin kings – over £17,000 for his reign covering 95 castles. The south of England needed protection from foreign invasion, hence John spent much on Dover, Rochester and Southampton (particularly at the latter after losing Normandy in 1204). In the west he spent over £1,400 on Corfe, much of this on the 'Gloriette' in the early years of his rule. He built Hanley in Worcestershire but tended to leave protection of the borders to the Marcher lords. In his second expedition to North Wales in 1211 he built or refortified perhaps ten to 14 minor castles (probably mainly earth and timber, mostly lost within two years). In the north castles were strengthened more against English baronial unrest than the Scottish threat. Despite rising prices, much money was spent on castles, especially as the political situation deteriorated. As his reign drew on John spent heavily on Lancaster, Scarborough and Knaresborough (more on the latter two than any others in his reign). By contrast costs for Launceston barely ever reached £20 during his reign.

Henry III spent approximately £85,000 on castle works during his reign, about £1,500 per annum or one 20th of his government receipts. In total £15,000 was spent on Windsor, over £10,000 on Welsh castles, £9,683 on the

Tower of London, £9,655 on Winchester and £7,500 on Dover. In the first ten years of his reign the royal guardians initiated a new hall at Winchester and upgrades at Rochester, Hertford, Lincoln, Devizes, the west curtain of Windsor, the Wakefield Tower at the Tower of London and a barbican at Bristol. Windsor, Winchester, the Tower, Nottingham, Marlborough, Bristol and Gloucester were also royal residences and so Henry lavished money on their decoration as well as defence, the cheapest outlay being Gloucester at £1,661. Over £10,000 was spent on Corfe during Henry's reign: 27,000 nails were bought together with 800 oaks and the same number of boards. £300 was spent on repairs to the donjon in 1235, while £62 went on partially replacing the palisades with walls. However, castles in outlying areas were often neglected unless the king happened to visit the area; even at York the motte received a new stone tower (Clifford's Tower) only when Henry arrived in 1245, some 40 years after the timber defences had blown down.

When Edward came to the throne there were no royal castles in north Wales. The Tower of London, Bristol, Chester, Dover, Leeds (Kent), Nottingham, Rockingham, Winchester and York were maintained for the king. Edward spent heavily on the Tower but also on Cambridge (to boost royal authority in East Anglia), Corfe (he completed the outer bailey of John), Rockingham and at Chester, and St Briavel's (new gateways). Conversely, castles on the Welsh borders such as Hereford, Bridgnorth and Shrewsbury, were no longer vital following the king's Welsh invasions, and were allowed to decline. Some castles in England were licensed to local barons, but these were often still allowed to fall into disrepair.

THE PRINCIPLES OF DEFENCE

The first line of defence in any castle was the ditch or moat. Many moats were dry because of the difficulty experienced in successfully diverting water from a river or stream. Some sites were naturally wet, which would result in the bottom of the ditch being boggy and partly filling with water during wet weather, enough to slow an attacker trying to cross it. Some ditch sides were revetted in timber or even in stone to make them smooth and difficult to climb.

The inner gatehouse at Beeston, Cheshire, part of the new castle built in the 1200s by Ranulf, earl of Chester probably in response to increasing royal power after the civil wars of John's reign. (Copyright English Heritage. NMR)

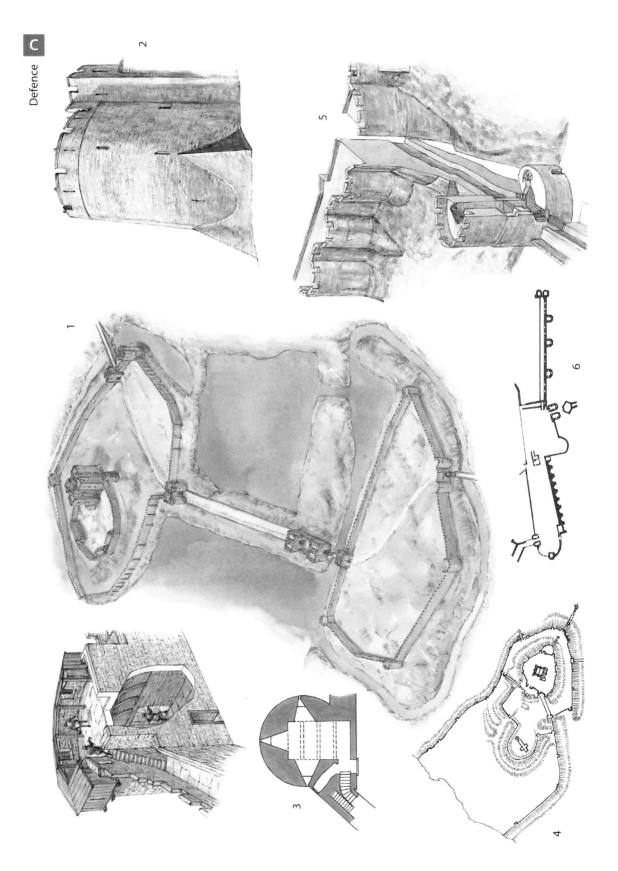

Bolingbroke, Lincolnshire, was a strongly fortified enclosure built by Ranulf at about the same time as Beeston. (Copyright English Heritage. NMR)

Timber stakes could be planted to slow attackers threading between them and make them easier targets. A few castles had enormous water defences, such as Kenilworth or at Caerphilly. However, some dry ditches are themselves quite formidable such as that at Beeston which was hewn from the rock.

The curtain walls of a castle provided the next obstacle. Some were built along the bank thrown up on the inner side of the ditch during excavation, which added height. A counterscarp or bank might also be raised on the outer rim of the ditch. Walls were invariably topped by a fighting platform: a wall walk and battlements consisting of solid merlons and gaps to shoot through, the crenels (hence the licence to crenellate, or fortify a place). Surviving merlons from the late 13th century at Chepstow in South Wales, together with some in North Wales and northern England, show that carved figures might be placed on the top of each. Merlons were sometimes provided with arrow loops and the crenels with pivoting wooden shutters to protect soldiers further on the wall walk. The inner side of the wall occasionally also had a low wall (parados).

The 13th century saw an increase in the number of mural towers set along the curtain to break it up and block movement for those reaching the wall heads. Wooden doors with bolts or drawbars usually controlled access from the wall walks. Other doors into towers were also defended; Marten's Tower

C DEFENCE

Kenilworth Castle as it may have appeared in the siege of 1266 (1). It stood on a spit of land that was surrounded by a lake some 45ha (111 acres) in area, with the approach along the rear of the spit protected by a dry ditch. Note that the modern castle has extra buildings and the moat is now grass. There is little surviving walling where the outer ward once stood.

Spur buttresses, as at Marten's Tower, Chepstow, presented solid masonry to an enemy (2).

Heber Tower (3) on the town wall at Newcastle also has stone corbels for a wooden hoarding. A projecting corbelled latrine (not visible here) was provided next to it and a turret a short way off. Open-backed mural towers, possibly closed by wood, were sometimes preferred to solid-backed towers.

Dover had its 12th-century concentric defences extended in the 13th century to seal off completely the ridge it commands (4).

After the siege of Dover in 1216 the vulnerable and damaged gate was completely blocked. Hubert de Burgh constructed a tunnel that emerged from the bank to a roofed section leading into St John's Tower in the moat with sortie doorways, then to an earthwork or spur (5).

The dam defences at Caerphilly (6) were built in two stages: the heavily buttressed south platform (left) is c.1268-71, with a watermill; the north platform is c.1277-90, complete with hexagonal barbican tower in the moat.

at Chepstow is a large example and every door in it originally had a portcullis running in slots up into the floor above. On rugged sites single towers are sometimes seen at salient points of the wall, such as at Montgomery.

Some towers were square but a few early in the century were octagonal to lessen the angles and so reduce the corner blind spot and provide fewer targets for a miner's pickaxe. Built in the 1230s by Hubert de Burgh, Hadleigh's polygonal bailey plan still had square towers at some corners, unlike his works ten years earlier at Skenfrith and Grosmont with their cylindrical towers (possibly as a result of cost). By this time most towers were D-shaped, curved to the field, or else completely cylindrical. In the late 12th or early 13th centuries an open-backed, timber-framed rectangular mural tower at Deddington in Oxfordshire was inserted into the motte during an overhaul of the inner defences. At Beeston the D-shaped inner curtain towers had solid backs, while the outer towers were open-backed but may have been closed with timber.

Towers were built out from the curtain and furnished with loops to enable the garrison to flay the face of the curtain with arrows or bolts. They were usually greater in height as well, so that they could overlook the curtain. Wall bases might be battered to thicken them and allow missiles dropped from above to bounce out. Goodrich has two forms of this strengthening around its towers, mirrored at Chepstow.

Command of the wall base was achieved by erecting wooden hoardings or brattices, shed-like structures projecting from the battlements and supported on great beams inserted through a line of slots (putlog holes) under the battlements. Gaps in the planked flooring allowed offensive materials such as stones, boiling water, pitch, red-hot sand, arrows or bolts to be showered down on to the heads of attackers. Loops were left in the front face of the hoardings to facilitate archers. However, being of wood they were vulnerable to fire so ideally should be daubed with clay or covered by rawhides but they could not withstand a heavy blow from catapults. Henry III built one along the battlements of the south front of the White Tower, overlooking the entrance door. The logical progression from the wooden hoarding was the expensive alternative of machicolation, bringing forward an entire section of battlements on stone corbels, with gaps between the corbels. When used, machicolations tended to be confined to gateways and some towers, but are less common in England than elsewhere in Europe.

The development of the gatehouse

At the beginning of the 13th century a gate might consist of a door through a wall with a mural tower beside it to protect it, such as the gate into the middle bailey at William Marshal's castle at Chepstow. Other castles had a single tower with an entrance passage running through it. The 12th-century version at Lincoln Castle's West Gate was heavily restored in 1233–34. Although both forms would continue into the later Middle Ages, gate defences were to improve beyond measure in the following decades, resulting in the most powerful gatehouses ever seen.

The idea of using flanking towers side by side to create a passage between them had already been seen at Dover in the 1180s, but such new ideas were not universally taken up for many years. After the failed siege at Dover by Prince Louis in 1216 an older tower was turned into a passage consisting of two D-shaped towers back to back. However, cylindrical or D-shaped towers were the usual form as twin-towered gates multiplied. Some of these early designs

were not so much towers as solid bastions. At the turn of the century de Warenne built such a gate on the north side of the town defences at Castle Acre, with another guarding the entry into the castle from the town. These each had two doors plus portcullises to block the passage, with a chamber each side of it.

Montgomery Castle was provided with a powerful gatehouse built in the ten or so years from 1224 and is one of the first in this style. Similar in date are the twin-towered gatehouses at Beeston in Cheshire and Bolingbroke in Lincolnshire, though their general layouts differ. Beeston's gates are the first of this design built by a baron, Ranulf of Chester, rather than a king.

A timber or stone bridge would span the moat or ditch, with a movable section by the gate. A few small castles may still have used bridges that were somehow run in, perhaps on rollers, when necessary. Others were lifted by chains that ran through telltale slots in the wall face into an upper room with a winch mechanism. Once vertical the bridge often fitted into a rebate in the wall.

The Island at Tintagel, Cornwall, contains early structures and was reached from the inner gate, whose ruins can be seen here. The Inner Ward lay beyond, with the walls of the Lower Ward visible behind. The latter led into the Upper Ward and out to the mainland. Much appears to be the work of Richard of Cornwall in the 1230s.

The walls and mural towers of the inner ward at Pevensey, Sussex, were probably the work of Peter of Savoy in the mid-13th century, though the twin-towered gatehouse could even date from the early years of the century.

Less common in England than Continental Europe was the bascule bridge, in which the bridge chains rose almost vertically to great wooden beams that ran back through slots in the wall, counterbalanced at the rear to assist lifting. However, quite a few castles made use of the turning bridge, which again utilized weights but this time attached at the rear of the bridge itself, which ran back into the gate passage. Removing pins allowed the weighted rear to pivot down into a lined pit while the front end swung up, thus presenting an additional obstacle. In some examples, only the long bridge beams (to which the planking was fixed) dropped into slots in the floor, or else the counterweights did, as at the Black Gate at Newcastle-upon-Tyne.

Thick wooden doors protected the passage, secured by drawbars that usually ran into slots in the stonework, although some turned on a central pivot. In addition, one or more portcullises could be added. The portcullis was a lattice, frequently of wood sheathed in iron but occasionally all metal,

D GATEHOUSES

The Constable's Gate at Dover (1), built by Hubert de Burgh between 1221 and 1227 to replace the old gate damaged by Prince Louis in 1216, was made by creating a passage through a cut-down tower of King John's reign (c.1205-14), protected by two D-shaped towers back to back. Adjacent towers gave flanking fire.

The early inner twin gate at Beeston of c.1220 has a single room across the first floor (2). A room below the gate passage reached by a stair from the west tower may have been a prison or just possibly a sally port or postern, in the same vein as under gatehouses in some south Welsh castles. The ruined outer gate was probably very similar.

The mid-13th-century gatehouse at Pembroke consists of a passage flanked by two rectangular towers but only one extends forwards to form a D-shaped tower (3). Two doors are each guarded by a portcullis and a *meurtrière*, a slot running across above the passage, with a third beyond the inner door.

The mid-13th-century Black Gate at Newcastle guarded the entrance to the castle through an angled passage (4). It had a turning bridge, whose counterweights fell into three slots, and flanking towers back to back.

The inner east gatehouse at Caerphilly (5) of c.1268–71 is a massive structure built by Gilbert de Clare and almost certainly inspired by his father's almost identical gatehouse at Tonbridge castle in Kent. A water chute from the room over the passage opened on the wall above the inner doorway for dousing fires. The towers either side were provided with latrines and a chapel, while a hall complete with hooded fireplace and window seats occupied the whole top floor, probably for the constable.

Unusually Goodrich (6) has one large flanking tower, with a chapel in the ground floor, but a much smaller tower the other side that held only a passage (far right) to a guard chamber at the front and latrine at the back but was furnished with a loop into the main gate passage. The turning bridge had three counterweights dropping into slots, then two doors with two portcullises between them. The portcullis chamber wall has cutaways to accommodate the winches of the first portcullis.

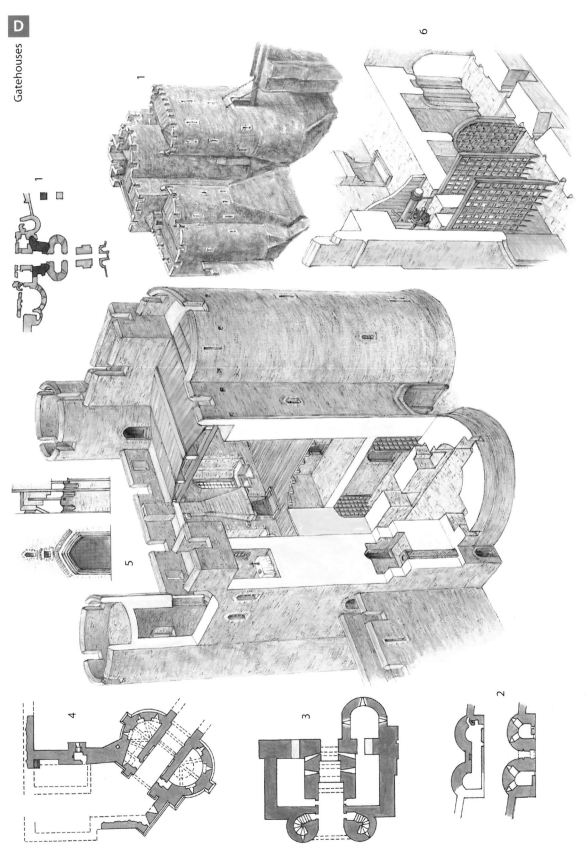

Clifford's Tower, York, a four-lobed tower begun by Henry III in 1245, sitting uneasily on the 11th-century motte, whose man-made structure caused the tower walls to crack.

running up and down in grooves in the wall. Very occasionally, as at Cooling in Kent, it ran over the outer face of the wall. In an emergency it was a matter of a few moments to release the winch and let the sheer weight drop the portcullis at speed. The area above the passage where the winch mechanisms operated could be made into one or more rooms by timber partitions. The gate passage itself was often vaulted or arched to carry timber floors that could be pierced by openings. These *meurtrières* or 'murder holes' as they are called, were most likely designed for pouring down cold water to douse fires started by an attacker, but there is no reason that offensive materials could not be loosed on to the heads of the unwary. The towers either side could be used to house porters and guards in time of peace, while garrison troops could use them to rush out on anyone breaching the defences. Some have loopholes opening into the passage as well as on to the outside.

The barbican

A barbican is a forework built in front of a gate to protect it. Occasionally of timber, only a small number of stone examples survive in Britain. The rebuilding of Oxford Castle after the siege of 1216 resulted in a D-shaped barbican being built, the ditch sides revetted in clay (gravelly soil). The rear wall was timber

The remains of the mid-13th-century lobated tower set around and enclosing the Norman motte at Pontefract Castle, West Yorkshire. The lobed design is somewhat similar to that at Clifford's Tower, York.

framed on horizontal timbers, as with the barbican at Chepstow. D-shaped open barbicans were used at the Tower of London (now concreted over) and Goodrich Castle, perhaps with lean-to buildings inside. Unusually, Sandal Castle was provided with a barbican in the bailey, a tower to guard the approach to the tower on the motte. The West Gate at Lincoln Castle was reworked in the late 12th or early 13th century and consists of two parallel walls jutting out from the gate but now modified on the north to form a rectangular platform some one metre long by half that in width; what it was for is not certain since only a very small catapult or spring engine could be sited here.

The gatehouse at Rockingham Castle, Northamptonshire, has been restored but retains much fabric of the mid-13th century flanking towers.

The postern or sally port

Sally ports are small openings that could be utilized instead of lowering the drawbridge and raising the portcullis of the main gate; they might also allow the garrison to make surprise attacks on besiegers or provide access for a messenger. Some were guarded by a portcullis as well as one or more doors. Many, as at Bolingbroke, consist of only a narrow door set in the curtain.

At Montgomery, the walls blocking the ditch between middle and inner wards had posterns, while Sandal had a postern in the western wing wall that linked the bailey to the motte. Knaresborough had a postern with a portcullis guarding the passage (some 27.5m) midway. Bristol had a tunnel (16m) opening out near the bottom of the ditch. Henry III's circular tower at Winchester Castle had a passage leading from the basement through a tunnel under the ditch to emerge in the city, while a second came out in the western suburb. Dover's tunnels, built by Hubert de Burgh after the 1216 siege, linked St John's Tower in the moat to a forward spur. He also built, on the eastern curtain, FitzWilliam Gateway with flanking towers en bec; designed mainly as a side gate or sally port, late in the century, the king was expected to use it if he arrived at night.

TOUR OF A CASTLE: THE TOWER OF LONDON IN THE 13TH CENTURY

In 1200 the Tower of London had already been in existence for about 125 years, a ditched and palisaded enclosure tucked into the south-east corner of the City of London and protected on the south and east by the old Roman city wall. Already in the later 12th century Richard I had expanded the castle

The Wakefield Tower, the huge cylindrical residential tower built by Henry III on what were then the outer walls of the Tower of London. Henry's water gate (later the heightened Bloody Tower) is just visible to the left. On the right the arch of Edward I's new water gate, St Thomas's Tower, spans the dock. It is connected to the Wakefield Tower by the Victorian reconstruction of Edward's bridge.

The Byward Tower (left) at the Tower of London, with a late medieval or Tudor second floor. It is the inner of Edward I's two gatehouses and connects via a causeway to the Middle Tower standing in the moat (the latter was partly resurfaced in Portland stone in the 18th century). To far right can be seen the slots for the counterweights of the turning bridge that guarded the now vanished barbican, the Lion Tower.

westwards and defined a new boundary. The Bell Tower remains at the south-west corner of this wall, its offset polygonal base made of marble to withstand the river water but with a cylindrical upper part.

Henry III expanded east and north, while Edward I turned the Tower into a powerful concentric castle, reaching its maximum size. The tour begins with the work of Henry. All the battlements visible today are 19th-century reconstructions.

In the 1220s, during Henry's minority, work began on a massive cylindrical tower probably on a Roman bastion and sited in what had been the south-west corner of the old Norman castle, before Richard's extension. This is the

Wakefield Tower, then known as the Blundeville Tower or Hall Tower. A second tower was also begun, probably the Lanthorn Tower (rebuilt in 1883–84) that is set at the south-east corner, the only mural tower with three floors rather than two. Both new towers were given chamber blocks that connected to a hall complex and may have been arranged for the king and queen. Henry certainly had rooms in the Wakefield Tower as well as the adjoining chamber. A curtain wall running north from the area of the Wakefield Tower, close to the original line of the Norman wall, turned east to meet the donjon (the White Tower) at its south-west corner. Foundations in the grass here show Henry's new inner entrance, Coldharbour Gate, with its D-shaped flanking towers leading into his private palace area. Today only the Wakefield Tower and rebuilt Lanthorn Tower remain; their chamber blocks are gone and the palace area is now laid to grass. Just west of the Wakefield Tower a water gate was built, the Garden Tower (now with a 15th-century upper floor and called the Bloody Tower after its questionable association with the later disappearance of the 'Little Princes', Edward V and his brother).

Seen from the outer ward, the postern gate in the inner east wall beside the Broad Arrow Tower, shows the ground level in the mid-13th century. (© The Board of Trustees of the Armouries)

In 1238 the Tower boundaries were pushed out northwards and eastwards with new curtain walls, so doubling the castle's area. The old Roman city wall running down to the Thames on the eastern side of the castle was now defunct and was probably dismantled; today only 'tramlines' in the grass within the castle indicate where it once formed the easternmost boundary of the Tower and indeed the City of London. Five powerful D-shaped mural towers were built along the new curtains. At the north-west corner is the Devereux Tower, then along the north side the Flint (rebuilt in the 19th century), Bowyer, Brick (also rebuilt) and Martin towers; down the eastern curtain are the Constable and Broad Arrow towers, with the Salt Tower at the south-east corner. A postern door is located on the outside of the Broad Arrow Tower but is now about 2.8m (nine feet) off the ground, since Edward I had the ground cut away and the foundations underpinned to heighten these towers when adding his outer ring in front.

A new gate tower was erected on the western curtain north of the Bell Tower, being on a line with Great Tower Street beyond. However, on 23 April 1240 the gate collapsed (as did a section of wall, probably nearby, a year later). Archaeology has revealed the footings of this tower. Henry ordered that the great donjon be given a coat of whitewash (no longer visible) and gave it the name it retains to this day – the White Tower. Downpipes were added to stop rainwater spoiling the new look.

E NEXT PAGE: TOUR OF THE TOWER OF LONDON

The plate depicts the Tower at its greatest expansion under Edward I, a huge concentric castle complete with wet moat and triple gate defences. At the heart of the complex stands the massive Norman donjon, the White Tower, which was still in use and now whitewashed by Henry III. King Richard's expansion west, marked by the polygonal Bell Tower at the south-west corner, allowed the original bailey south of the donjon to become a private ward for the king and queen, entered via Coldharbour Gate. Henry III pushed the new castle boundaries north and east with new curtain walls, before Edward added an outer ring.

The new gate defences of Edward I begin with a half-moon barbican, the Lion Tower, from which access was afforded to the Middle Tower within the moat and thence the Byward Tower, which also had a postern. Access between the inner and outer walls was also controlled by partition walls.

Edward increased the firepower of the western inner wall with a powerful line of embrasures commanding the ground beyond and making use of the slope to the lower outer wall. They were supported by the great bulk of the Beauchamp Tower, which replaced the old gatehouse.

Edward's new water gate, St Thomas's Tower, allowed boats to moor directly in the basin within its walls. The old water gate (in use before Edward claimed the land from the river for his new walls, and later named the Bloody Tower) stands behind on the inner walls, flanked by the cylindrical Wakefield Tower, part of the private royal lodgings.

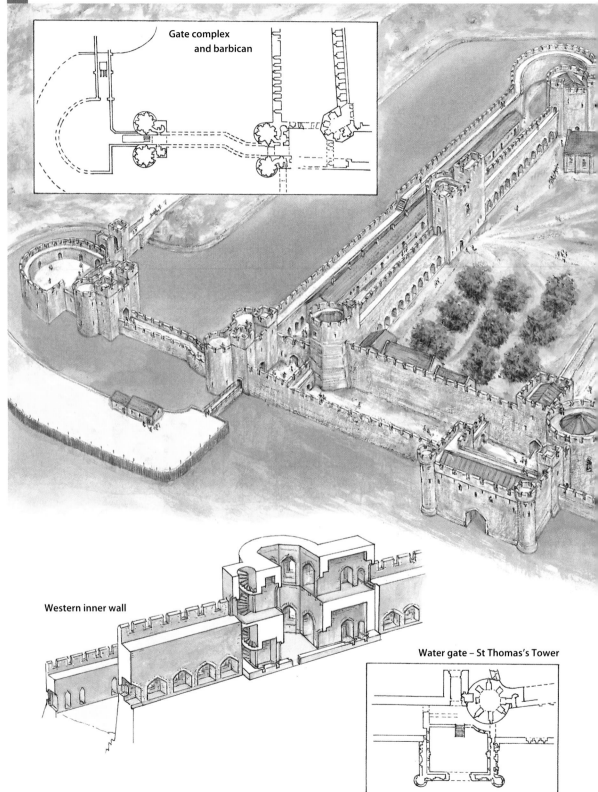

Gate complex and barbican

Western inner wall

Water gate – St Thomas's Tower

Richard I

Henry III

Edward I

Edward I expanded the castle into a concentric fortress (a rarity in England) with a triple gatehouse defence and a new water gate. The work cost a staggering £21,000, more than twice the amount spent by his father. The first item was a new wet moat. This was 50m (160ft) or more in width and was fed from the river using sluices to control the level. So enormous was the work that the diggers and hodmen were paid £4,150 over the six years from 1275 until 1281. The moat became so fetid over the centuries that it was drained in the 19th century and today we see a grassy ditch, the original bed in the centre being about 4.5m (15ft) further down. Entry into the castle was via a newly sited triple-gateway complex at the south-west corner, completed in 1281. The moat extended around the first obstacle, a semicircular open barbican called the Lion Tower because it became the site of the royal menagerie of wild animals. Pulled down in the 19th century, no trace remains above ground, although archaeological excavation in 1999 revealed some foundations. Originally a causeway protected by a spur gate led across the moat to the barbican via a turning bridge whose weighted inner beams dropped into slots; these and the pit spanned by the bridge can be seen. A left turn through a 90-degree angle within the barbican led on to a causeway that ran a short distance across the moat to the first gatehouse, the Middle Tower. Standing within the moat, this gate is flanked by cylindrical towers and was guarded by a turning bridge, portcullis and doors. From here the causeway (originally with high walls set with loops – only the lower part of the south wall survives) continued across the moat, gave a slight kink and then reached the main curtain, here protected by a second great twin-towered gatehouse, the Byward Tower, slightly taller (the second floor is later) and timber backed (the present timber is not the original). Unlike the Middle Tower, a portcullis remains but the turning bridges have been replaced by a modern extension of the causeway. A postern gate is on the river side just east of this gatehouse (made into a tower called the Byward Postern in the 14th century). From the Byward Tower the way led into the outer ward between the outer and inner walls, the south side being Water Lane.

Edward's outer ring of walls was lower than it is today to allow a field of fire for archers on the inner curtain. There were few towers on this outer ring: the north-west corner has a bastion called Legges Mount, at that time level with the low outer curtain, while the east wall had three rectangular bastions immediately south of the north-east corner, possibly for siting siege engines. The northernmost was somewhat disrupted when another bastion, Brass Mount, was added to this corner, partly of brick and fitted with multiple loops accessed from a gallery. At the same time all the outer walls and bastions on the landward side were heightened, possibly because of fitting in the Royal Mint buildings.

Down at the south-east corner of this outer curtain the rectangular Develin Tower is a 15th-century replacement for Edward's. Returning west along the river side is the L-shaped Well Tower, also probably Edward's work. The ground floor vaulted chamber has two stone-lined chutes presumably used for drawing up water. Further west the gateway called the Middle Drawbridge probably marks the position of another of Edward's postern gates. Westwards along the river the existing outer wall is of 14th-century date. However, the new outer wall had meant reclaiming the area from the river, which effectively ended the Wakefield Tower's role as a water gate. Across from it Edward I therefore built a new river gate, St Thomas's Tower, with a remarkably wide arch allowing boat access into a small dock inside with steps up. Originally the distance from the inner curtain to this dock was only about three metres (ten feet) but it latterly gained ground at the expense of the dock area. A mural

St Thomas's Tower on the outer south wall of the Tower of London. The water gate (latterly renamed Traitors' Gate) is now half hidden by the wharf that was extended from the western end of the Tower in the 14th century under the supervision of Geoffrey Chaucer. St Thomas's Tower was restored by Anthony Salvin in 1864–66.

passage either side ran round the walls at ground level, providing access to numerous loopholes and rooms in the cylindrical south-west and south-east corner turrets, whilst above were a hall and chamber with surviving fireplaces and possibly a chapel in the east turret. The portcullis mechanism was probably on the roof. This gate would later become known as Traitors' Gate. A bridge (now a Victorian replacement) connected the north-east turret to the upper chamber in the Wakefield Tower. Cross walls and gates were added between the inner and outer walls near the Bell Tower, St Thomas's Tower and Salt Tower, to further block access; these have all now vanished except for the partial remains of one connecting the Salt to the Well Tower.

On completion of the new gates the massive D-shaped Beauchamp Tower was built on the site of Henry's collapsed gate on the western inner curtain. Internally Flemish brick was used in the largest number so far discovered in England. On either side the curtain itself was rebuilt (also partly using brick) as a formidable firing platform, the rear pierced at ground level with a long line of embrasures (these now hidden behind Tudor and Stuart buildings) allowing missiles to be loosed *en masse* from both this and wall-walk level.

In the north-west part of the inner ward, near Tower Green, the Chapel of St Peter ad Vincula was refurbished by Henry III but rebuilt by Edward I in 1286–87. The Victorians revamped it in the 19th century.

Finally a postern for foot traffic was added to the City wall north of the Tower moat, since the latter's construction would have caused some demolition of the wall. Originally of three storeys, the postern's partial ground floor and basement are visible near the modern pedestrian underpass.

THE CASTLE AT PEACE

Much of a castle's life was spent at peace. Odiham in Hampshire was built by John in 1204 so he could 'disport himself' in the forest, while Restormel in Cornwall, despite its battlements, has large windows rather than arrow loops. Castles were ideal for storing records and became centres for the dispensation of local government and for shire courts. The king's representative, the sheriff, often had his seat in a castle within a town, backed up by soldiers if necessary.

The walls of the Bishop's Palace at Wells, Somerset, built by Robert Burnell, Bishop of Bath and Wells and friend of the royal chancellor, in 1285, are provided with cylindrical corner towers and a wet moat.

The hub of a castle was its hall, used for eating, sleeping (for some), entertaining and business. In 1241 the hall at Windsor Castle and that in the donjon were used as reception areas to feed the poor on Good Friday. As here, larger fortresses might have two halls, one for the lord's inner circle and one for public use. Those found in gatehouses were almost certainly for use by the constable during his lord's absence.

Timber halls continued in use, perhaps with one or two aisles (rare in western Britain). Aisles widened a hall either allowing a continuation of the roof or by use of a pitched or lean-to roof of their own. Walls could be infilled with wattle and daub, or staves, planks or posts. Timbers might be raised on dwarf stone walls to prevent the wood from rotting from contact with the earth. Timber partitions could supply smaller rooms.

Stone halls increased and their cost indicated the rank of the owner. At Conisbrough the hall (c.1202–40) had four bays supported on octagonal pier bases. Earlier stone halls might be expanded. Sometimes repair work was necessary, as at the mid-century hall at Hadleigh (17 × nine metres) only some 50 years later, owing either to collapse or earth movement. As well as adding a central line of eight timbers resting on pads, external buttresses were

F DOMESTIC ARRANGEMENTS

The now ruined 'Gloriette' at Corfe (**1**) was a residential suite built by King John between c.1201 and 1204. It comprised a first floor hall of four bays above a vaulted undercroft, reached by a stair via the north end where there was a presence chamber (or possibly a chapel). At the south end and set at right angles to the hall, a door led into a long chamber above a barrel-vaulted undercroft. Corfe had six or seven suites.

Roger Bigod III's domestic range at Chepstow (**2**) uses the slope of the ground. A transverse service passage leads into the large single-storey kitchen, with serving hatch. The high wooden roof probably had a louvre or similar in the centre to take smoke from a central hearth (the existing oven is later). A doorway led out northwards to the riverside wall and probably to a platform and then stairs up to the top chamber of the block that is sited at the eastern end of the kitchen. The lowest room of this block was entered from the bailey, which also had a door into the prison in the adjoining gatehouse. The two upper chamber rooms each had a latrine and decorated windows. A vaulted porch led into the eastern end of the hall, the doorway decorated with two painted

shields each hanging by a painted ribbon from a nail. A more central doorway in the service passage led up steps towards the hall with the buttery (right) and pantry (left), with a second set below. On the other side of the entrance passage a doorway led down steps, firstly to a landing with access to a platform overlooking a narrow cleft in the rock beside the river, then to a vaulted cellar with another opening similarly overlooking the creek; supplies could be winched up via a pulley whose floor bracket survived into the 19th century.

The hall at Goodrich (**3**) ran along the west curtain, the lower end connecting to the South-west Tower housing the buttery and pantry (divided by a timber partition). The kitchen lay beyond, on the south side. The north end of the hall had a lobby and the North-west Tower formed a complex with the first-floor solar block on the north side.

Plan of the late-13th-century shell keep at Restormel (**4**). The chapel just from the circular walls on the right, with the lady's chamber above and lord's below. Next to the latter is the hall, separated from the kitchen by a servery.

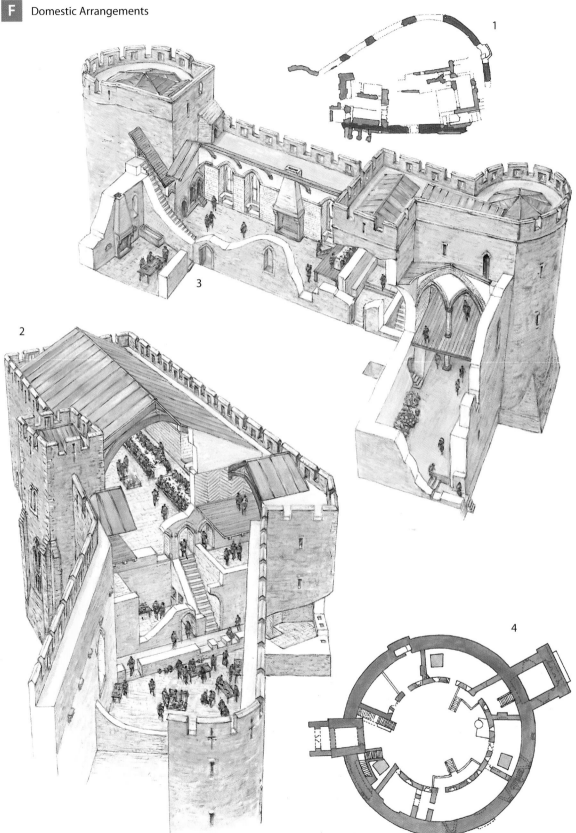

1

3

2

4

The rectangular fortified manor at Acton Burnell, Shropshire, built by Bishop Burnell in the late 13th century. The building consists of a rectangular domestic block with angle turrets and a projection in the middle of its west end; a chapel once stood in the larger north-east turret. The battlements are low and give the illusion of strength but there is little chance the castle could have withstood anything but a raid.

supplemented on the inside by others (on the surviving east wall), in an attempt to stave off the imminent problem. By the end of the century the hall was in danger of collapse and may even have done so; a new hall was built with its west side on the old east wall. When Sandal's new first-floor stone hall was built the old timber hall was utilized to house workmen building the stone castle.

The size of a hall varied, from the modest late-13th-century rebuilt hall at Hadleigh (11.4 × 6.6m.) to the early-13th-century halls at Skenfrith (25.6 × 6.75m) and Conisbrough (22 × nine metres), both of which used a curtain wall to save construction costs, although security limited window size. By 1300 there was an increasing desire to increase interior area by removing aisle posts; the weight was instead taken by cruck roof timbers, supported on corbels and helped by collars and braces. Fragmentary infill in the upper half of a truss at the late-13th-century ground-floor hall at Stokesay suggests this was to help vector smoke up to a louvre. Windows here were glazed only in their upper half, with shutters to keep out draughts in the lower part. One of Sandal's windows shows an internal slot for a shutter.

There were two halls at Launceston. One was a single-storey timber-framed building, with clay floor and a hearth at one end; it was probably the administrative building but later became a workshop before being renovated, with replastered walls and seating along the wall. The great hall lay some 20m north-west, set over an earlier structure, with wall benches and a hearth near the dais; it was transformed into a first-floor structure with solar.

The late stone hall at Rumney had a roof of sandstone slabs and glazed earthenware ridge tiles, while the solar at Hadleigh was probably roofed in lead or shingles.

The modest late-13th-century enclosure at Stokesay was mainly built by Lawrence of Ludlow, a highly successful wool merchant, who began work in about 1285 but died in 1296 before it was completed. It has a curtain wall that originally rose to a height of about 11m (35ft) from the bottom of the moat, while the gatehouse was replaced in the 17th century. Inside the walls the buildings consist largely of a stone hall and chamber block, with a tower at each end; the north tower is now crowned with a Jacobean jettied upper storey that may have replaced a similar structure.

Chambers

By the 13th century there was an increasing use of private chambers by the lord and his intimates. In the lower bailey at Windsor new royal apartments were linked to a chapel via a cloister that enclosed a lawn, complete with a stone bench near the king's chamber. Royal nurseries were built for the baby Prince Edward (born 1239) and his sister, whilst at Old Sarum (Salisbury) there was a nurse's chamber. At Winchester Henry III had a chamber provided for his stewards (between hall and kitchens), plus chambers for his knights, the chaplain and priests. In some cases these facilities were repeated in order that the family might retain their own quarters.

In the second half of the 13th century the first-floor hall at Sandal was flanked by new quarters. Entered from the hall, east and west chambers each stood over a vaulted undercroft supported by a single pillar. The Privy Chamber to the north was quite possibly a chamber for latrines. North again lay the constable's lodgings, near the gate as is quite often seen, since the constable controlled a castle in the lord's absence. The latter and his kin resided in the donjon on the motte. Hadleigh's mid-13th-century chamber was L-shaped around a small courtyard, with plastered walls and glazed windows (red fragments were found).

Domestic arrangements underwent rebuilding as taste and money dictated, as at the ground-floor hall at Stamford, with four piers (two and two) and a hearth. Around 1200 a first floor was added to the solar, the hall was slightly narrowed, then the east end was extended, now with an arcade east wall (to a screens passage?) and the southern pair of pillars were removed. A porch was built on the north-east side in the 14th century.

Henry III added additional wooden accommodation such as the chamber and wardrobe complete with fireplace in plaster for a visiting bishop. Such buildings might be connected to the permanent rooms by numerous passages but were vulnerable to fire and so layouts could change regularly.

The main beds might be made in sections to allow for transport. On 18 November 1296, 2d was itemized for five frames for the pavilion over the bed of the Countess of Pembroke during her visit to Goodrich. The wardrobe was a storage room not only for clothes but for anything of value: plate, jewellery and even the imported and often expensive spices, or the prized

Richard FitzAlan is probably responsible for heightening the earlier gatehouse at Arundel, Sussex, in the later 13th century and adding the powerful barbican to protect it.

The internal domestic buildings at Restormel, Cornwall, are set against the outer walls. The well is set below the antechapel with modern steps up to the large opening into the chapel. To left and right of it are the lady's and lord's chambers respectively; to right of the latter is the hall. The kitchen (not visible here) has a door and hatch into a servery, from which another door and hatch allowed food to be passed to those carrying it via an external roofed stairway to the hall.

powdered sugar perhaps flavoured with spices or flowers. These would be kept under lock and key and parcelled out as necessary to the castle cook; some sugars were treated as medicine, as prescribed by Master Hugh of Evesham for Edward I's son together with liquorice.

Decoration

Restormel had been plastered and limewashed to be even more effective, and this was seen in a number of castles. Comfort and colour in royal accommodation is much in evidence, especially under Henry III. At Winchester the queen's chamber was painted green, while at Windsor the wainscoting in one of the queen's chambers was green with gold stars, the cloister walk decorated with paintings of the Apostles. King Henry ordered whitewashed walls and a ceiling of green with gold and silver spangles in the great chamber at Guildford Castle; the pillars and arches in the donjon were marbled. In 1236 a glass window in the gable of the queen's chamber in the upper bailey at Windsor was painted with the Tree of Jesse and two other windows glazed and shuttered (the chamber was nevertheless rebuilt the following year). The nurseries at Windsor were two-storeyed timber buildings west of the queen's lodgings and built around a courtyard; in 1239 that of young Prince Edward was wainscoted and provided with iron bars to stop anyone gaining access. At Winchester the chamber for the king's knights was vaulted and wainscoted. Even the king's seat in the great hall there was repainted, together with doors, windows and the pictures above the dais. Bishop Robert Grosseteste thought that (with a view to allegory and symbolism) green, blue and red were the proper colours for the ideal castle.

In 1250 the 'table' by the king's bed was to be painted with images of the guardians of Solomon's bed, the chambers of the king and queen to be paved with tiles, wooden windows to be made in the gallery of the queen's chapel, the privy chamber before the door of the Jew's Tower repaired and similarly the long chamber above the stables in the tower where the wardrobe was usually made (Liberate Rolls). Henry was constantly issuing orders for new latrines or the repair of old ones. Baths are mentioned twice at Odiham under the countess of Leicester. Great barons also enjoyed colour and comfort.

The South-East Tower at Goodrich Castle, Herefordshire, showing the great spurs to thicken the base of a castle already sitting on a rocky site.

At Marlborough a writ to the constable of 1241 shows that even the cellar before the queen's chamber was to be provided with a fireplace, the walls wainscoted and whitened and a window provided that was to be painted with a dove and barred with iron.

Kitchens

Some buildings may have been chambers or kitchens, since a range of hearths can, without other evidence, be interpreted as either. As at Conisbrough, the kitchen might be situated in a separate building to minimize the risk of fire. Timber walls were weatherboarded instead of being the usual wattle and daub construction. At Launceston the kitchen was separated from the hall by a yard; a capped and slate-lined drain led out across the clay floor.

Kitchens were often upgraded (often on the same site) throughout a castle's working history. In 1244 two kitchens were built at Ludgershall, one being earmarked for Henry III whenever he visited the castle. These seem to have replaced the kitchens mentioned under King John, with ovens large enough to roast two or three oxen. Eynsford retained its 12th-century kitchen when a new one was built. The cob-walled kitchen at Wallingford (c.1200) was 12.5 x 8.5m, consisting of three rooms with hearths in the floor of compacted earth, clay and sand, the central room being the largest; a new kitchen was built separately in 1228–29. If curtain palisades were rebuilt in stone, service rooms might be moved against them, as at Sandal, which had a late 12th- or early 13th-century malthouse with kiln for drying the corn, overlaid in the first half of the 13th century with a new single-storey kitchen (about 10.4 x 9.4m) with bakehouse to the west and larder to the east. All had hearths (including unusually the larder), and the kitchen hearth had post holes presumably for spit supports. The kitchen also has evidence of a drain linked to an open culvert, thence flushing into the barbican ditch. The bakehouse (which is possibly later in date) was divided by a cross-passage from the doorway into three areas by timber partitions, with two ovens in its eastern part and two larger ones to the west. Montgomery had a brewhouse, built of timber on dwarf walls, with a tank for soaking barley; paving nearby would be for laying the barley out to germinate afterwards, after which it would have been transferred to a small kiln for drying.

The great hall at Goodrich can be seen at centre, with a doorway from the courtyard and internal doors leading into the buttery and pantry in the South-West Tower beyond. The foundations of the kitchen can be seen to the right of the Norman donjon, while the doorway to its left led down into a vaulted prison (with a drawbar hole on the outside of the door!)

The shingle on the roof of the great kitchen was removed in 1260 when the constable was ordered to replace it with lead; however, the shingle was to replace the thatch lately taken off the roof of the outer chamber in the high tower.

One of three dovecotes at Richard's Castle may possibly be of 13th-century date and was situated below the castle on the town bank. The dovecote at Winchester stood behind the queen's chapel. A new dovecote was ordered to be erected by the castle at Marlborough in a writ to the constable dated 1241.

Okehampton had a cistern (2.5m deep) cut in the rock at the base of the motte (12th–13th centuries). It probably had a roof, or some form of protection, supported by walls on two sides. The well at Beeston is over 100m (110yds) deep and perhaps as much as 146m (160yds), with masonry to 61m (200ft), making it the deepest well in an English castle. A now-lost piped water supply may be the answer in some castles where no obvious well or cistern exists. At Goodrich washbasins set in walls around the castle (often near gateways) were provided with piped water from the well.

The ditch at Odiham was naturally marshy and partly filled with water, which led one enterprising custodian to ask the king for a licence to fill it with bream, ideal for fast days. The King's Pool, the artificial lake at Clifford's Tower, was used as a fishpond and the river Foss drove watermills.

The high arches and central pillar of the solar block at Goodrich, now without its flooring. A vestibule stood behind the arches, with the North-West Tower beyond. To the left is the great hall with access from the courtyard into the lobby area by the angle with the solar.

Chapels

Most castles had a chapel and possibly a more private one for the lord's use. At Winchester Castle the queen's chamber was provided with a beam on which was set a cross flanked by figures of St Mary and St John, while St Christopher bearing the infant Jesus and St Edward giving his ring to a pilgrim were painted on the western gable. The Liberate Rolls recall that in December 1250 an instruction was sent to the sheriff of Hampshire saying that the king's new chapel at Winchester was to be painted with the story of Joseph and floored with tiles. A marble altar was installed in King Henry's chapel and a new privy chapel built near his bed. As at Harlech and Caernarfon, the chapel at Clifford's Tower in York is over the gate and has the portcullis rising into it but this may have been a conversion to religious usage, with arcading brought from a chapel in the bailey at the end of the century. At Goodrich the chapel at the side of the gate has a drawbar hole in the wall for the bar closing the main gate next door; records of 1297 show it was also used to store oats.

Workshops and pens

Castles needed a number of workshops to enable them to function. A blacksmith or farrier was essential given the number of horses to be shod and the metal items to be made or repaired. Larger castles would have an armourer to repair armour and weapons, though items of quality would be bought elsewhere. Stables were a necessity though little survives from the period. Probably most were timber built, with stalls and provision for the stable boys, tack and food. Henry III provided a chamber with three beds and the harness by the stables at Winchester. Barns and a granary held food for the castle; storage areas had to be available in case of siege or in case the owner, be he king or baron, arrived with his retinue to stay for a while. Chickens were consumed in quantity and eggs were used in great numbers in cooking and thus poultry must have graced a castle, though additional supplies could be obtained from outlying manors and farms. At Christmas 1206 a command went out to the sheriff of Hampshire for 1,500 chickens, 5,000 eggs, 20 oxen, 100 pigs and 100 sheep for the royal table. Pens could hold cattle, sheep and pigs. Kennels were built especially in castles near royal hunting areas, supervised by dogkeepers.

Gardens and parks

Castles might well have a garden for private use by the lord and his family. Tintagel under Richard of Cornwall (or possibly earlier) had on the island section of the castle a quadrilateral walled enclosure about 23 × 15m (75 × 50ft), in which slabs set on edge marked paths running some two feet from the walls with another cutting in half the central bed. So windswept was this site on the coast that potted plants had to be brought over when Richard came to visit.

The park at Ludgershall Castle was ditched and hedged in 1244. In 1261, Henry III wrote asking his chief gardener to buy pear trees to plant in the strip

The 'Gloriette' at Leeds, Kent, was built by Edward I after acquiring the castle in 1298. The private royal suite sits on a small island accessed via a covered bridge from the main castle, which also stands in the large moat. The upper floor and large windows are Tudor additions.

of land beyond the tower moat (kept clear for defence), lately enclosed by a mud wall. At Conwy, Roger le Fykeys, a squire serving the queen, was paid 3d for watering the new lawn in front of her chamber (made from turves specially sent up the river and fenced with barrel staves) one evening in July 1283.

Prisons

Castles are inextricably associated with prisons and dungeons. Bishops' castles such as the one at Wells could be used to house ecclesiastical prisoners incarcerated whilst awaiting a hearing (which could take years!), unlike laymen who received summary justice after trial. A prison for women, with a chapel over it, was built in the bailey at the royal castle of Clifford's Tower in York between 1237 and 1241. A prison (no sexual preferences mentioned) also formed part of the new building there begun in 1245.

Castles also held political prisoners, including men awaiting punishment for treason or those captured in battle awaiting ransom. Prince Edward was held at Wallingford after the battle of Lewes in 1264. A small party of loyalists broke into the outer ward but Edward himself ordered them to dissipate when the threat was made to send him back by mangonel (he subsequently escaped the following year). Unscrupulous kings and noblemen could and did sometimes ignore the laws – hence the clause in the Magna Carta of 1215 specifying that no freeman will be held prisoner without trial. John notoriously flung his scheming nephew Prince Arthur into Corfe Castle, where he was castrated and blinded, subsequently dying from his wounds. Arthur's sister, Eleanor, was kept in comfortable confinement until her death in 1241 after 40 years a prisoner in Bristol Castle or occasionally Gloucester. John's cruelty also fell upon William de Braose's wife, son and daughter-in-law, by all accounts starved to death in Windsor. In 1212 he hanged 28 young Welshmen imprisoned in Nottingham Castle in retaliation for the Welsh seizure of royal castles and their decapitation of knights and other soldiers. However, in 1203 another of John's prisoners, Saveric de Malleon, apparently managed to break loose and actually blockaded himself in the donjon at Corfe. The records of Old Sarum suggest that breakouts were not that uncommon.

It is worth remembering that most window bars were designed to stop people climbing in. The attempted breakout of Llewelyn ap Gruffydd from the Tower of London by sliding down knotted sheets went wrong when it broke and he plummeted to his death. It should be noted that this suggests he was not kept in a 'dungeon' (derived from 'donjon', the great tower). In a different twist, in 1233 two garrison sergeants rescued Hubert de Burgh, shackled in Devizes Castle, one night to save him from being murdered by the jealous bishop of Winchester.

The inner gate and D-shaped towers of White Castle, seen from the outer ward, were probably added to the 12th-century walls either in 1263 or 1267–77 by the Lord Edward. The entrance was re-orientated from south to north.

THE CASTLE AT WAR

Many castellans were often royal officials, holding royal castles. However, some of these men began to regard the position as hereditary, and cause problems if the monarch challenged their title. Philip Mark, sheriff of Derby and Nottingham, dragged his heels when the royal council wanted to remove a deputy from the bishop of Lincoln's castles of Sleaford and Newark. The coronation in 1220 of the young Henry III required a baronial oath to surrender royal castles and wardships if required and to help crush those who refused (especially entrenched foreign barons). However, some castellans had held fortresses loyally for John for years and were well regarded by their English peers. The king might also wish to take over private fortresses.

Garrisons were chosen from either feudal rotas or hired men. Castle-guard was part of the feudal agreement and as such a man invested by his lord agreed to discharge service in his lord's castle (or one of them) for a set number of days per year. Service was usually 40 days in war or in peace but this could be commuted to a money payment for the hiring of mercenaries; in John's reign this often meant crossbowmen. However, Magna Carta states that 'no constable shall compel any knight to give money instead of castle-guard if he is willing to do the guard himself or through another good man'. It also takes sheriffs and royal bailiffs to task for obviously having bullied free men to give up horses and carts to carry materials for castle work, nor are they to take their timber for castle or other works without agreement.

Siege engines might be held in castles, such as the mangonel and petrary sent to Corfe Castle by order of King John in 1214. Some of these machines were kept in storage, larger items in sections, so they could be taken wherever they were required for service.

Both John and Henry III suffered civil wars and each reign demonstrates the formidable resources even relatively weak kings could muster against such threats. Ultimately rebel factions could not bring enough force to bear against royal power, despite seizing castles. Neither was the king prepared to sit and starve out the rebel defenders, nor were the defenders cowed into surrender by the size of the royal forces before them.

The Black Gate was added to the castle at Newcastle-upon-Tyne in about 1250. It consists of two D-shaped towers back to back to form the passage, which took a right turn at the rear over another ditch and drawbridge. Three slots in the floor took the counterweights of the main turning bridge. The upper part is not original work.

Rear view of the gatehouse at Tonbridge, Kent, built by Richard de Clare, probably the model for the work of his son, Gilbert, at Caerphilly.

King John

In 1215 the rebels renounced fealty to John and attacked Northampton Castle, which held out for two weeks until the besiegers, lacking siege engines, grew tired and withdrew to Bedford followed by London. King Philip Augustus of France even sent over a renegade monk, Eustace, with engines to assist the rebels. John, having brought over foreign mercenaries, began to move on his enemies and sent forces to raise the sieges at Northampton and Oxford.

The king turned towards Rochester in Kent. After seven weeks a mine collapsed one corner of the donjon but the defenders held out temporarily

G THE SIEGE OF BEDFORD, 1224

Falkes de Bréauté refused to comply with royal requests to yield up castles and moved to Bedford Castle with his brother, William. Falkes had strengthened the Norman motte and bailey, enlarging the area, revetting ditches in stone and erecting new curtain walls and a new donjon on the motte. On 17 June William seized a royal justice, Henry de Braybrooke, and led him into Bedford Castle accompanied by over 80 soldiers. Braybrooke's wife rushed to Northampton and alerted Henry.

The king wasted no time mobilizing and a messenger appeared at the castle to demand surrender but William replied that he answered only to Falkes. Henry flew into a temper and swore to hang the entire garrison. He moved to Newport Pagnell where, on 20 June, he sent orders for crossbow bolts, equipment for siege engines, pickaxes for miners but also wine for his household. He arrived at Bedford later that day.

Within eight days supplies for the engines began arriving then the engines themselves: some from Lincoln by 7 July; mangonels from Oxford and engines from the sheriff of Northamptonshire. The Dunstable Annalist describes two mangonels on the western side 'which wore out the old tower' plus one each to north and south, both causing a breach in the walls. On the eastern side was a petrary and two mangonels whose purpose was to direct their missiles against the keep each day.

A regular bombardment of the castle was met by crossbow bolts that killed at least one of the knights, many soldiers and

those working around the machines. Two huge siege towers were erected, from tall trees around Warden Abbey and nearby woods. The constant pounding by the catapults began to cause areas of wall to crumble.

The first assault was aimed against the barbican, which was taken with minimal losses to the besiegers. However, the second attack to seize the outer bailey was stubbornly resisted and, though the object was achieved, it resulted in many casualties on both sides. The mine under the inner curtain was fired and the wall above collapsed. Royalist troops made a determined surge through the breach but the inner bailey was stoutly defended and a hail of missiles dispatched many attackers. A number of besiegers launched themselves at the donjon but failed to gain entry; instead ten of them were dragged inside.

Henry's miners drove their tunnels under the foundations and, on 14 August, fired the props. Although the tower did not collapse, a disconcerting crack appeared in the walls and smoke billowed into the rooms. Obviously shaken by this turn of events, the rebels released Henry of Braybrooke and the other prisoners plus all the women, amongst them the wife of Falkes de Bréauté himself. Having attempted to negotiate, the garrison marched out the next day and surrendered, hoping for mercy. However, Henry was obviously out to make an example and ordered 80 rebels to be hanged.

behind the cross-wall of the donjon before surrendering. So impressive was this victory that no other castle offered serious resistance. Troops were set about London to watch the rebel headquarters but, perhaps unwisely, there was no assault to end the revolt. John progressed via Nottingham north to Berwick, with various towns and castles opening their gates to his harrying army of mercenaries along the way: Rockingham, Belvoir, Pontefract, York, Richmond, Durham, Warkworth, Alnwick and Berwick, the latter stormed on 15 January 1216. He marched into Scotland in reprisal for Alexander III's siege of Norham (19 October to late November) and then turned south, receiving the surrender of Skelton, Fotheringay, Bedford and Framlingham. In Essex Colchester surrendered on 25 March 1216 after a very short siege while Hedingham castle yielded in three days. John also took Hertford.

When Louis landed with French forces in May he captured Reigate, Guildford, Farnham, Winchester, Odiham, Marlborough and Worcester. Odiham, with its octagonal and buttressed donjon, had a small but spirited garrison that sallied out on several occasions, in one incident seizing 13 prisoners.

Louis fruitlessly besieged Dover from July to October. Despite using a mine to collapse part of one gate the breach was stoutly defended by Hubert de Burgh and his men. To add to Louis's problems many loyal castellans refused to betray their king; Barnard Castle successfully held out against the Scots and one of the rebel leaders, Eustace de Vesci, was killed during the siege. Durham stood firm, while Windsor also resisted rebel troops.

Beginning in November, Louis took Hertford, and then besieged Berkhamsted, the large motte and bailey castle now with stone walls. The castle held for two weeks despite a pounding from the besiegers' engines. After Berkhamsted was taken, Colchester, Orford, Norwich, Cambridge, Pleshey and Hedingham followed.

Meanwhile John, driven from Winchester, organized his defence plan from Corfe and recruited troops in the west before striking east in mid-September. He moved past Windsor to draw away its besiegers, laid waste to the Isle of Axholme and then approached and entered Lincoln, the castle held by the widow of Gerard de Camville, Nicholaa de la Hay, who, says the Barnwell annalist, had freed herself from the siege by a money payment. John then organized supplies for his northern castles, prompting the king of Scots and northern rebels to leave the siege of Dover. Louis raised the siege and returned to London but the French threat receded following a royalist sea victory off Sandwich. However, John died at Newark Castle on 18 October.

Henry III

In spring 1217 Louis returned but the Marshal had all the captured castles dismantled. Louis promptly went to Winchester, restored the tower and walls and repaired the breaches, setting the Count of Nevers in charge of a strong garrison. Meanwhile Gilbert de Gant had seized the city of Lincoln but its castle was bravely defended by Nicholaa de la Hay. The royalist earls of Derby and Chester had besieged Montsorrel in Leicestershire but by the time a rebel force approached the siege had been lifted, so they turned to assist in the siege of Lincoln Castle. The castle sits in the south-western corner of the Roman city walls, which still survived except on the south. On an eminence within the city walls was a space between castle and cathedral where the besiegers had concentrated. William Marshal heard of this development while at Northampton. Nottingham, Newark and Sleaford castles held royal mercenaries and now Marshal detoured from Newark (where gathered

406 knights, some 200 sergeants and 317 crossbowmen) and made for Lincoln. As he approached, Gilbert fled. On 20 May the royalists arrived from the north-west early in the morning and entered the castle via the western wall, where no rebel troops had been posted. Falkes de Bréauté prepared to sortie from the eastern (inner) gate of the castle. The Bishop of Winchester spotted a blocked-up gateway further north along the Roman west wall; this was opened up and the royalists poured into the space between the castle and cathedral, catching the rebel besiegers gathered there. William Marshal ordered that the crossbowmen shoot at the horses, which tumbled to earth, leaving their riders to be taken prisoner. The onslaught sent the Frenchmen and rebels reeling down Steep Street into the city and in the mêlée the count of Perche was killed. A swinging door in a narrow gate held up the retreating troops and when a cow was jostled into it the whole access was blocked, resulting in many prisoners. The Roman north gate was seized and counterattacks by the rebels thrown back. Some 406 royalist knights together with men-at-arms and 317 crossbowmen had captured 300 enemy knights and put the other 300 to flight. The soldiery sacked churches and houses, smashing open chests and cupboards.

Despite a royalist sea victory that effectively ended the French intervention, Louis was still paid off with a huge bribe to go home in September, ending the civil war. Hubert de Burgh declared Henry to be of age in 1220 and demanded the return of castles. The earl of Aumale shut the gates of Rockingham but it was captured, so he took two other strongholds, which resulted in fighting, his excommunication and banishment. It took ten days for 12 carts loaded with parts for siege engines to traverse the roads to the siege of William de Forz at Bytham in Lincolnshire; at 16km (ten miles) per day it was about half the speed of the rest of the army, but William surrendered. In 1224 Falkes de Bréauté refused to give up Bedford Castle but it fell after a vigorous siege by the young king, which cost £1,311 18s 2d.

War in Wales

In 1223 the justiciar, Hubert de Burgh, led an army to relieve Builth and begin a new castle at Montgomery (granted in 1228). By 1231 Hubert controlled Grosmont, Skenfrith, White Castle, Cardigan, Carmarthen, Brecon, Abergavenny, Radnor and others. Llywelyn revolted, having lost the lordship of Builth. The garrison in Montgomery Castle, close to the pillaged lands, set out to quash the Welsh. Blocking their escape, the English killed some and captured others, who were executed by order of Hubert. Llywelyn sent a monk to lure out the garrison with a tale that Llywelyn and a small force

Looking north across the lake towards the walls of Caerphilly, showing the great expanse of water an attacker had to negotiate before encountering the two lines of walls. (By kind permision of Anthony de Reuck)

The eastern gatehouses at Caerphilly (1268–71). Much of the low outer concentric walls are rebuilt, as are the outer faces of the inner gatehouse towers. Note the Leaning Tower slighted after the English Civil Wars but rebuilt much as it once looked.

could be reached by fording the river. The Welsh drew back towards a wood as the leading horsemen sank up to the horses' bellies in the mud and were set upon by the Welsh. Llywelyn harried from Montgomery to Radnor, Brecon and Caerleon, then south-west to Cardigan Castle. Hubert brought a royal army to Painscastle, on the road to Hereford, but waited months while a stone fortress was built to replace the old Broase Castle. His campaign of Elfiel (near Builth) was thus a fiasco and a truce was made with Llywelyn. A truce made in 1234 allowed him to keep Cardigan and Builth.

In 1233 King Henry came to the siege of Richard Marshal in Usk and achieved results by asking, through bishops, that Richard yield up the castle to preserve his honour and he would receive it back in 15 days. Richard did so, only to find that royal honour did not stretch to keeping faith!

Llywelyn died in 1240 and the following year Cardigan and Builth were retaken by royalist forces. His son David's failure to come to arbitration ended in Henry invading Wales; he had built a castle on the rocks at Dyserth near Rhuddlan and decided to rebuild Deganwy. However, he had to pull out. On David's death in 1246 Henry now managed to make peace with the latter's nephews, Llywelyn and Owain but in November 1256 Llywelyn attacked the Four Cantrefs. In 1258 he assumed the title 'prince of Wales'.

While Henry was in France Llywelyn besieged the Lord Edward's castle at Builth in January 1260 and meanwhile took fire and sword into south Wales and attacked Abergavenny. In 1262 he attacked Mortimer and overran Brecon. The Welsh tenants of the Marcher lords rose up and Llywelyn captured Edward's castles in the north. Using siege engines and a small fleet from Ireland, Llywelyn destroyed Dyserth Castle and recovered Deganwy in 1263. The Treaty of Montgomery ended hostilities in 1267. Edward returned from Gascony, supplied Deganwy and Dyserth with mercenaries but lost them to the Welsh later that year, since no help came from the Marcher lords.

The Barons' War

English discontent found a focus initially in Prince Edward's steward, Roger Leyburn, and this self-interested group found a leader in Simon de Montfort. Despite the king's return war broke out, initially in the Welsh Marches. Henry of Montfort was pushed back by Edward and tricked himself into Gloucester town but not the castle. Robert de Ferrers marched south and stormed Worcester, hoping to meet up with those in Gloucester, but on 5 March Edward was back in Gloucester Castle. The baronial army was gathering in Northampton and Henry, joined by Edward at Oxford, struck out for Northampton. On 6 April 1264, helped by friends inside Northampton, Edward burst into the town and the following day the castle surrendered.

Henry moved towards Nottingham and Edward harried in Derbyshire and Staffordshire. The royal constable, Roger de Leybourne, held Rochester. On 17 April Gilbert de Clare moved from his castle at Tonbridge and approached from the south or west. In response the garrison fired those suburbs lying towards Canterbury and also burned the king's hall in the castle (probably on the premise that a controlled fire now was better than an uncontrolled one later). Simon de Montfort meanwhile moved from London and came through Strood, only to be beaten back at the Medway as his troops arrived at the crossing place. After a second failed attempt he finally appears to have sent a fireship loaded with pitch, coals, sulphur and fat bacon against the bridge on 18 April, using the chaos (or smoke) to cover his force as it crossed, presumably over the fording place. A pre-arranged assault by Simon and Gilbert then captured the city in the early evening, their men looting church plate and destroying valuable records, while mounted men chased their enemies actually into the cathedral. The following day, 19 April, Simon's forces broke into the bailey and the garrison pulled back into the great donjon, now repaired since its partial collapse in the siege of 1215. The next day being Sunday, hostilities were suspended but on Monday siege engines were brought up and vainly battered the tower for a week. In the end the news that King Henry and Prince Edward were approaching caused Simon and Gilbert to retire and the siege was lifted on Saturday 26 April.

The king found the castle badly damaged but nothing was done about it; indeed, soon afterwards, constables were being accused of pilfering stone for their own use, while in 1281 permission was given to demolish the hall and chambers that had been burned so the stone could be re-used in the castle. However, the place remained a decaying site until major rebuilding was undertaken in 1367.

After Simon de Montfort's death at Evesham in 1265 resistance continued at Ely, Axholme and Kenilworth, where water or marshes made all three difficult to approach. Kenilworth, a strong castle in a marshy landscape with formidable water defences consisting of a 45ha (111-acre) lake formed by damning two steams, had been rather irresponsibly given to Simon de Montfort by Henry in 1254. Now it was held by his son and namesake who

brought in additional troops and went out to rally sympathizers, since royal forces did not arrive to challenge him until the spring of 1266. As a gesture of goodwill he released the king's brother, Richard of Cornwall, and agreed peace terms but the garrison was swelled by local men and refused to give in. To make matters worse a royal envoy had his hand cut off, which broke the rules of war. Simon the younger had dallied in the priory at Kenilworth and was surprised by Edward outside the castle. Despite escaping inside, most of the barons and knights with him were captured.

Henry arrived and set up camp on land now occupied by the town, where was brought the Sword of State. The archbishop of Canterbury excommunicated the garrison but this was rebuffed when a surgeon dressed in suitable garments appeared on the battlements and 'excommunicated' the king, archbishop and the royal army. Henry refused to leave in order to attend his daughter's wedding at Windsor and the marriage took place in the siege lines at Kenilworth.

Siege engines were set up on the north, south and east sides because of the width of the lake elsewhere and catapults began to bombard the fortifications as best they could. The defenders replied by lobbing missiles at the enemy catapults, which we are assured frequently collided in midair with those of the besiegers. When this bombardment proved relatively ineffective an assault was sent across the dry ditch but this had no more success than had the barrage. An amphibious assault, using boats sent from Chester, was launched across the lake but this also failed. To add to the discomfort of the besiegers the garrison launched several sorties to damage siege engines and cause mayhem, and their catapults managed to smash a belfry called 'The Bear', which was being used to overlook the castle and allow archers to pick off those working the catapults. By October the castle had still not been captured so lenient terms were drawn up in a council at Coventry but were rejected when offered. The frustrated king summoned forces from Northampton to put an end to this troublesome fortress with an all out assault, but before this could be done disease broke out in the castle, probably typhoid, and it was this silent killer that finally broke the garrison's will. They submitted on 12 October, using a clause in the original agreement that they could surrender within 40 days. Henry now enjoyed a period of peace until his death in 1272.

The gateway into the Upper Bailey from the Barbican (1219–45) at the western end of Chepstow Castle. A small postern gate is let into the wall on the right.

It is interesting to note that the number of sieges during the Barons' War was lower compared to the conflicts of John's day, thanks largely to the improvements in the defences and increased use of stone walls.

Edward I

The peace established with the destruction of the Montfortian party continued in England under its new king until the end of the century but in the borderlands peace remained elusive. Wales refused to submit to English directions and finally Edward led the first of his armed interventions in 1277 and a second in 1282. His massive castle-building programme and dealings with the Welsh princes has been covered in another volume in the series. A third Welsh war broke out in 1293 but ended the following year and by 1297 Edward had control of Wales and now marched into Scotland. He spent the rest of his reign trying to deal with this neighbouring kingdom, becoming known as the 'Hammer of the Scots'. Castles along the borders, as in Wales, were always on the alert for raids and at certain times for full-scale invasions by the Scots. Carlisle on the west coast and Berwick on the east found themselves on the front line and Berwick, together with its walled town, would change hands numerous times in its history. In the lowlands, the royal siege in 1300 of the triangular Caerlaverock Castle became the celebrated subject of a detailed poem that rather distorts the actual importance of the event itself.

AFTERMATH

During the two centuries after 1300 there was no significant growth in the number of castles. England and Wales were already thick with fortresses, though there were times when it seemed prudent to consider building new ones. While England might seem more settled, the threat from Scotland would

The outer gatehouse at Chepstow, Gwent, dates between 1219 and 1245. Marten's Tower on the left (1270–1300) has huge spurs to deter mining.

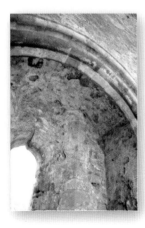

remain real until at least the 17th century while Welsh unrest remained constant. France too remained a danger, especially after the outbreak of the Hundred Years War in 1338. After that war ended in 1452 England drifted into the Wars of the Roses but, despite the potential power of most castles, they figured relatively little in the politics of the day and military conflict tended to be settled on the battlefield rather than by siege warfare. In any case improved gunpowder meant different forms of defence were becoming desirable. New, more comfortable tower houses appeared that had much less defensive strength than earlier designs. Many castles had further work done to them although this was often the addition, or the rebuilding, of domestic ranges to provide more comfortable accommodation at a time when large manor houses were becoming an increasingly attractive alternative.

In the 16th century military emphasis was being concentrated on forts designed to house artillery. These were low with thick walls to deflect enemy cannonballs but did not have suitable accommodation for a lord so were not castles in the true sense of a residence. Some castles were converted to suit increased residential use. Chepstow had a number of windows, doors and fireplaces inserted into the walls against which were built new buildings for the household of the earl of Worcester; similarly the gatehouse had large windows inserted. By contrast, Castle Rising is reported even in the later 15th century as in decay so the mention of Tudor visits suggests the guests made use of newly built housing there; these guests included Mary, sister of Henry VIII and ex-queen of France, and her husband, Charles Brandon. Similarly, Rockingham was in such poor repair by 1485 that Henry VII had a hunting lodge put in the park. Edward Watson turned the castle into a Tudor mansion in 1544. In the 16th century Beeston had already developed the legend that the castle would rise to save England one day and a further legend developed of the treasure of Richard II being hidden in the inner well (a short tunnel does lead off the shaft).

Many castles saw their last stand in the English Civil Wars and fell foul of the improved power of gunpowder, or were afterwards slighted by Parliament to prevent their being used again. Despite becoming a Tudor house, Rockingham's strength was noted and Royalists fortified the donjon. The castle suffered severely in the siege and subsequent capture by Parliamentary forces. It was gradually restored following the war. In the 19th century Anthony Salvin 'improved' its medieval appearance (not least by adding castellation), as he did at the Tower of London and other sites.

In 1643, Parliamentary forces laid siege to Corfe Castle but despite a bombardment and assaults the garrison lost only two men in contrast to over 100 lost on the Parliamentary side. By October 1645 Corfe was besieged again. Lady Bankes refused the chance to escape offered by loyalists who got through enemy lines and the castle fell by treachery, when soldiers disguised as reinforcements were allowed to enter. Parliament voted for its demolition the following year. Chepstow was also bombarded in 1645 and again in 1648 during the second Civil War. Four cannon soon knocked a hole in the walls and prompted many of the royalist garrison to surrender before the anticipated attack came. After the Civil War Chepstow became a barracks until 1685 and a prison for political prisoners.

Goodrich was captured by Parliamentary troops in 1646 partly as a result of the water supply being cut off and the castle was slighted. Pontefract underwent three sieges during the Civil Wars, between 1644 and 1649, and was noted as particularly powerful by Cromwell himself. However, despite the structure surviving generally, it was deliberately demolished after the third siege, becoming a complete ruin; only the main guard in the barbican escaped, to be used as a debtor's prison and to house French prisoners of war in 1673. In the later 19th century it became a pleasure park complete with romantic ruins.

Launceston was already becoming run down by the time of the Black Prince's survey in 1337, which lists roofless or disjointed buildings and a prison that was almost useless; 16 years later the mayor and bailiffs were ordered to stop pigs trampling down the moat as it was likely to cause the walls to fall down! Work was done to make the castle at least usable for judicial business but again it was so derelict following the Civil Wars that it was not even considered necessary to slight it. Already in 1650 houses and gardens had sprung up in the ditch between the town and castle. As with others, its role as a prison remained in the form of the North Gatehouse,

BELOW LEFT
Barnwell, Northamptonshire, built by Berengar le Moine in 1264–66, taking advantage of Henry III's civil wars. (By kind permission of Anthony de Reuck)

BELOW RIGHT
The rectangular stone enceinte with four cylindrical corner towers at Kidwelly Castle was probably begun by Pain de Chaworth in about 1275.

where the constable had his quarters. Henry III's aisled hall at Winchester was peaceably taken over in the 17th century for administration of the law.

In the 18th century demolition was suggested for the now-decaying castle at Rochester but abandoned because of the difficulty, followed by an unsuccessful attempt to turn it into a government barracks. In the 19th century it was converted into a pleasure garden although the remains of the gate to the city were destroyed in the process and a new entrance knocked through. However it did result in repairs being carried out generally. Dover remained a front-line stronghold, modernised in the 18th and 19th centuries, with its underground tunnels seeing service during World War II.

VISITING THE CASTLES TODAY

Acton Burnell, Shropshire (English Heritage)
About 13.4km (8.3 miles) south of Shrewsbury off the A458. Take the left turn at the village crossroads; access is a very short walk through a wood. A solitary gable end from a 13th-century hall in nearby private grounds is said to be the site of the first English parliament.

Allington, Kent (Private)
Turn north-east some four kilometres (2.5 miles) north-west of central Maidstone off the A20. Remains of late 13th-century enclosure walls, towers and gatehouse, restored tastefully in the early 20th century.

Arundel, Sussex (Duke of Norfolk)
15.9km (9.9 miles) north-west of Worthing off the A27. Late 13th-century enlarged gate and barbican, strengthened 12th-century walls and a shell keep remains but much else dates from 1870–90.

Bamburgh, Northumberland (English Heritage)
On the B1341, some 26.7km (16.6 miles) north-east of Alnwick off the A1. Situated on a cliff but accessed from the village, where the Grace Darling Museum can also be visited. Best viewed from the beach below. Henry III built the gatehouse.

Barnard Castle, County Durham (English Heritage)
In the centre of town, 27.8km (17.3 miles) west of Darlington on the A67. The Bowes Museum is nearby.

The delightful small castle of Manorbier, Pembroke, begun by the de Barris in the 12th century, was strengthened in the next century by John de Barri.

Barnwell, Northamptonshire (Private)
3.8km (2.4 miles) south of Peterborough, east of the A605.

Bedford, Bedfordshire (Beds County Council)
The castle was destroyed following the siege of 1224 and only the damaged motte remains, much of the bailey being built over. Bedford Museum is next to it, with displays concerning the siege.

Beeston, Cheshire (English Heritage)
About a mile west of the A49, some 17km (10.6 miles) north-west of Nantwich. Large spectacular site but fairly ruinous castle.

Berkhamsted, Hertfordshire. (English Heritage)
Eight kilometres (five miles) west of Hemel Hempstead off the A4251. Large motte and bailey with remains of stone walls.

Bolingbroke, Lincolnshire (English Heritage)
At Old Bolingbroke, off the A155 about 5.6km (3.5 miles) north-west of West Keal. Largely foundations remain.

Brough, Cumbria (English Heritage)
35.1km (21.8 miles) south-east of Penrith off the A66. 13th-century domestic buildings and heightening to donjon.

Brougham, Cumbria (English Heritage)
On the B6262, 1.8km (1.1 miles) south of Penrith on the A66. Mainly the inner gatehouse survives from the 13th century.

Caerphilly, Mid Glamorgan (CADW)
12.4km (7.7 miles) south of Cardiff off the A469. Huge 13th-century concentric castle with 14th-century hall, set within massive water defences complete with fortified dam platforms.

Castell Bryn Amlwg, Shropshire (Shropshire County Council)
22.5km (14 miles) south of Montgomery off the B4368. The castle is now mainly an earthwork close to the Welsh border.

Chepstow, Gwent (CADW)
Off the A48 and about 4.3km (2.7 miles) from the M48. Extensive ruins set on top of a cliff.

Clifford's Tower, York (English Heritage)
In the city near the east bank of the river Ouse, on a huge motte.

Corfe, Dorset (National Trust)
6.9km (4.3 miles) south-west of Wareham on the A351. Best reached by parking on the village outskirts and walking through the village.

Dover, Kent (English Heritage)
Massive castle on the eastern outskirts of town off the A2. If using a car, be prepared for queues approaching the town and port. Alternatively, walk or taxi from Dover Priory station in the town. Most battlements have been lost.

Goodrich, Herefordshire (English Heritage)
6.8km (4.2 miles) south-west of Ross-on-Wye off the B4234.

Grosmont, Gwent (CADW)
17.5km (10.9 miles) on the A4347, north-east of Abergavenny via the A465 and Groesonen Road. A first-floor hall is set within curtain walls.

Hadleigh, Essex (Essex County Council)
Near the Hadleigh Castle Country Park between Hadleigh and Benfleet, about one kilometre (0.6 mile) south of the A13 and 9.1km (5.7 miles) west of Southend-on-Sea.

The gatehouse at Warkworth, Northumberland, was built in the early 13th century and heightened probably in the second half of the century. Machicolations overlook the doorway, with holes for the beams of hoardings around the twin towers. The remains of the contemporary semi-octagonal Carrickfergus Tower are on the left.

Hopton, Shropshire (Private)
Small rectangular donjon about 12.1km (9.4 miles) north-west of Shrewsbury off the A5.

Kenilworth, Warwickshire (English Heritage)
On the B4103, 8.1km (5.1 miles) south-west of Coventry off the A429, on the western outskirts of Kenilworth. Large castle with early ruined gatehouse but the water defences are now dry. There is also a Norman donjon and the 14th-century hall of John of Gaunt.

Kidwelly, Dyfed (CADW)
14.9km (9.3 miles) north-west of Llanelli. A square curtain with corner towers and an outer ring wall on the landward side.

Launceston, Cornwall (English Heritage)
34.5km (21.5 miles) north-west of Bodmin, close to town centre on the A388. A shell keep and tower stand on the motte.

Lincoln, Lincolnshire (Lincolnshire County Council)
In the city centre. Large bailey with two mottes, much already built by 1200. Good views of the cathedral.

Ludlow, Shropshire (Earl of Powis and Trustees of the Powis Castle Estate)
About 38km (23.6 miles) north of Hereford off the A49. 13th-century towers added to the curtain surrounding a 12th-century donjon and chapel, and 14th-century domestic block.

Manorbier, Dyfed (Private but open)
About 9km (5.7 miles) south-west of Tenby on the B4585. Mainly 13th century, with gardens inside.

Middleham, North Yorkshire (English Heritage)
17.5km (10.9 miles) south of Richmond off the A6108. Late 13th-century walls, modified later, enclose a large Norman donjon.

Montgomery, Powys (CADW)
About 12km (7.5 miles) from Welshpool off the A483. The castle ruins are up a steep slope on the west side off the town square.

Newcastle-upon-Tyne, Tyne and Wear (City of Newcastle)
In the centre of the city, off the A69. The railway passes very close to the donjon. The Black Gate (gatehouse) has a bagpipe museum. The town walls can be traced.

Oxford, Oxfordshire (Oxford Castle Heritage Project)
On the east bank of the river, off the A4144. Subsequently grew into Oxford Prison but now part of the Malmaison hotel complex; the castle can be visited.

Pembroke, Dyfed (Private Charitable Trust)
About 17.7km (11 miles) south of Haverfordwest off the A4139. The castle is set above the river to the north-west of the city centre. It is largely of *c.*1200 with a huge cylindrical donjon.

Pevensey, Sussex (English Heritage)
8.4km (5.2 miles) north-east of Eastbourne on the B2191. The Norman castle within the Roman fort was strengthened in the 13th century with a towered curtain and gate.

Peveril, Derbyshire (English Heritage)
On southern outskirts of Castleton, 16.3km (10.1 miles) east of Buxton off the A6187. 13th-century hall was placed in a corner of the Norman castle.

Pickering, Yorkshire (English Heritage)
28.2km (17.5 miles) west of Scarborough off the A170. 13th-century shell keep on a Norman motte, with work of various periods.

Pontefract, West Yorkshire (City of Wakefield Metropolitan District Council)
17.3km (10.8 miles) east of Wakefield off the A645; turn off at Broad Lane for Castle Chain. Large but fairly ruinous castle enclosure.

Restormel, Cornwall (English Heritage)
1.6km (one mile) north of Lostwithiel on west bank of river Fowey. The domestic buildings are inside the circular shell keep.

Rochester, Kent (English Heritage)
In the centre of town, by the river Stour facing Bridge Reach. The repaired corner of the huge donjon, damaged by King John's miners, is best seen by walking round the road outside the castle.

Sandal, Yorkshire (City of Wakefield Metropolitan District Council)
About 3.7km (2.3 miles) from Wakefield, just off the A61. Now much ruined. Provides a view of the battlefield of Wakefield (1461).

Skenfrith, Gwent (CADW)
19.9km (12.4 miles) north-east of Abergavenny on the B4521. The castle is relatively unspoiled.

Stokesay, Shropshire (English Heritage)
11.7km (7.3 miles) north-west of Ludlow on the A49. Picturesque small castle or manor house, with moat and 17th-century timber gatehouse.

Tintagel, Cornwell (English Heritage)
About 9.7km (six miles) north-west of Camelford on the B3263. Spectacular site on the cliffs but very ruinous.

Tiverton, Devon
23.7km (14.7 miles) north of Exeter off the A396. Rectangular late 13th-century castle with two surviving towers, a 14th-century gate and some later work.

Tonbridge, Kent
8.5km (5.3 miles) north of Royal Tonbridge Wells off the B2260 (High St). The three-storey gatehouse and Norman motte with shell keep survive.

Tower of London (Historic Royal Palaces)
No parking facilities except a multi-storey paying car park. Nearest Underground is Tower Hill on the Circle and District Line. The Crown Jewels are also displayed in the Tower, which can become very busy in the summer months.

The remains of the barbican tower of *c*.1270 (left) at Sandal, Yorkshire, which stood inside the bailey and led across the ditch where the ashlar facings of the ruined D-shaped towers guard the stairs up the motte. The postern can be reached from the ditch.

Tretower, Powys (CADW)

14.1km (8.8 miles) north-west of Abergavenny off the A479. 12th -century shell keep with 13th-century cylindrical donjon set inside it. Near the castle is later medieval Tretower Court.

White Castle, Gwent (CADW)

12.1km (7.5 miles) north-east of Abergavenny off the B4521. 12th-century walls have 13th-century towers and a gatehouse.

Winchester, Hampshire (Winchester City Council)

The castle, now the home of the County Council, is on the south side of the B3404 at the top of the High Street. The great hall remains, now a museum where can be seen the 'Round Table'. Outside is a reconstructed medieval garden. An excavated circular mural tower from the city wall is visible nearby.

Windsor, Surrey (The Royal Collection)

Walls and mural towers of Henry III survive on the west side of the castle and south of the motte. Two baileys and work of various periods, especially the 19th century.

BIBLIOGRAPHY

In addition to the works cited, excellent guide books are available for many of the castles in England from English Heritage and for many Edwardian castles in Wales from CADW, the Welsh tourist board.

Amt, E., 'Besieging Bedford: military logistics in 1224', *Journal of Medieval Military History*, 2002, Vol.1, pp. 101–24

Ashbee, Jeremy. '"The Chamber called Gloriette": Living at Leisure in Thirteenth- and Fourteenth-Century Castles', *Journal of the British Archaeological Association*, 157 (2004), pp. 17–40

Baker, David and Evelyn, 'Bedford castle excavations', *Bedfordshire Archaeological Journal*, Bedfordshire Archaeological Council, 1979, vol. 13, 1979, pp. 7–64

——, 'Bedford Castle', *Castle Studies Group Journal* 2005–6, Vol. 19, pp.127–29

Beresford, M., *New Towns of the Middle Ages* (Lutterworth Press: London, 1967)

Bradbury, J., *The Medieval Siege* (The Boydell Press: Woodbridge, 1992)

Brown, R. Allen, *English Castles* (2nd ed., Batsford: London, 1976)

——, *Castles from the Air* (Cambridge University Press: Cambridge, 1989)

Butler, Lawrence, *Sandal Castle, Wakefield* (Wakefield Historical Publications: Wakefield, 1991)

Clark, G. T., *Medieval Military Architecture in England* (Wyman & Sons: London, 1884)

Colvin, H. M., R.A. Brown, and A. J. Taylor, (ed.) *A History of the King's Works, The Middle Ages*, 2 vols (HMSO: London, 1963)

Davies, R. R., *Conquest, Coexistence, and Change: Wales 1063–1415* (Oxford University Press: Oxford, 1987), reprinted as: *The Age of Conquest: Wales 1063–1415* (Oxford University Press: Oxford, 1991)

——, *The Revolt of Owain Glyn Dŵr* (Oxford University Press: Oxford, 1995)

Edwards, G., 'Edward I's Castle Building in Wales', *Proceedings of the British Academy*, 32 (1947), 16

Gies, Joseph and Frances Gies, *Life in a Medieval Castle* (Abelard: London, 1975)

Goddard, A. R., 'The Great Siege of Bedford Castle', *Bedfordshire Times* (1906, reprinted 1985)

Greenshields, Margaret, 'The siege of Bedford castle', *Bedfordshire Magazine*, vol. 4, pp. 183–90

Guy, John, *Kent Castles* (Meresborough Books: Rainham, 1980)

Harvey, Alfred, *Castles and Walled Towns of England* (Methuen & Co: London, 1911)

Kenyon, J. R., *Medieval Fortifications* (Leicester University Press: Leicester, 1990)

Kenyon, J. R., and R. Avent, (eds.), *Castles in Wales and the Marches; Essays in honour of D.J. Cathcart King* (University of Wales: Cardiff, 1987)

King, D. J. C., *The Castle in England and Wales* (Croom Helm, 1988)

——, 'The defence of Wales', *Archaeologia Cambrensis*, vol. 126 (1977), pp. 1–16

Labarge, M. W., *The Baronial Household in the Thirteenth Century* (The Harvester Press: Brighton, 1980)

McAleavy, Tony, *Life in a Medieval Castle* (English Heritage: London, 1998)

McNeil, Tom, *Castles* (B T Batsford/English Heritage: London, 1992)

Morris, John E., *The Welsh Wars of Edward I* (Alan Sutton: Stroud, 1997)

Morris, Marc, *Castle: A History of Buildings that Shaped Medieval Britain* (Macmillan: London, 2004)

Neaverson, E., *Medieval Castles in North Wales: a Study of Sites, Water Supply and Building Stones* (Liverpool University Press, Liverpool, 1947)

Oetgen, J., 'A regeneration issue: Bedford Castle Mound', *The Archaeologist* (2005) Vol. 57, pp. 12–14

Parker, Mike and Paul Whitfield, *Wales – The Rough Guide*, (Rough Guides Ltd: London, 1994)

Parnell, Geoffrey, *The Tower of London* (B T Batsford/English Heritage, London, 1993)

Pettifer, Adrian, *Welsh Castles* (The Boydell Press: Woodbridge, 2000)

——, *English Castles, A guide by counties* (The Boydell Press: Woodbridge, 1995)

Platt, Colin, *The Castle in Medieval England and Wales* (Secker & Warburg: London, 1982)

Pounds, N. J. G, *The Medieval Castle in England and Wales* (Cambridge University Press: Cambridge, 1994)

Powicke, Sir Maurice, *The Thirteenth Century, 1216–1307* (Oxford University Press: Oxford, 1962)

Prestwich, M., *Edward I* (Yale University Press: London, 1997)

Rickard, John, *The Castle Community. The Personnel of English and Welsh Castles, 1272–1422* (The Boydell Press: Woodbridge, 2002)

Roberts, Ian, *Pontefract Castle* (West Yorkshire Archaeological Survey: Wakefield, 1990)

Salter, Mike, *The Castles of The Thames Valley and The Chilterns* (Folly Publications: Malvern, 2002)

Sorrell, Alan, *British Castles* (William Clowes & Sons Ltd: London, 1973)

Taylor, A. J., 'Master James of St. George', *English Historical Review*, LXV (1950), pp. 433–457

——, *The King's Works in Wales, 1277–1330* (HMSO, 1974)

——, 'Castle-Building in Thirteenth-Century Wales and Savoy', *Proceedings of the British Academy*, 63 (1977), pp. 265–92

——, *Four Great Castles: Caernarfon, Conwy, Harlech, Beaumaris* (Gwasg Gregynog Ltd, Newtown, 1983)

——, *Studies in Castles and Castle-Building* (Hambledon Continuum: London, 1985)

——, *The Welsh Castles of Edward I* (The Hambledon Press: London, 1986) This previously as 'The King's Works in Wales' in Colvin above.

Thompson, M. W., *The Rise of the Castle* (Cambridge University Press: Cambridge, 1991)

——, *The Decline of the Castle* (Cambridge University Press: Cambridge, 1987)

Toy, Sidney, *Castles, Their Construction and History* (Constable: London, 1985)

Warner, Philip, *Sieges of the Middle Ages* (G. Bell & Sons Ltd: London, 1968)

Warren, W. L., *King John* (Eyre Methuen: London, 1978)

GLOSSARY

Apse	A rounded end.
Ashlar	Smooth, flat masonry blocks.
Bailey	A courtyard.
Ballista	A projectile engine resembling a giant crossbow, utilizing the tension of a bow or the torsion of two arms thrust through skeins of cord. Usually for shooting large arrows or bolts.
Bar hole	A hole in a wall into which a drawbar slides.
Barbican	An outwork that protects a gate.
Barrel vault	A cylindrical plain stone vault.
Bascule bridge	A bridge lifted by chains suspended from counterweighted beams.
Batter	The base of a wall thickened with a sloping front.
Belfry	A wooden tower, often mobile, used either to overlook a wall or to transfer troops on to it.
Berm	The space between a wall and ditch.
Brattice	Wooden hoarding built out from a battlement to command the base of a wall.
Buttress	Stone support built against a wall to reinforce it.
Corbel	A supporting stone bracket.
Countermine	A tunnel dug from a castle aimed at breaking into an enemy mineshaft.
Counterscarp	The outer slope of a ditch.
Crenel	The open section of a battlement.
Crenellation	Battlement.
Cross-vault	A vault in which two barrel vaults intersect.
Curtain	A length of wall surrounding a castle or town.
Daub	A filling used to cover wattle walling, made from mud or clay sometimes mixed with dung and straw.
Donjon	A great tower or keep, but it can also refer to an upper bailey or lord's private area.
Drawbar	A wooden beam for securing the inside of a door, which runs back into a hole in the wall to allow the door to open.
Embrasure	An internal opening in a wall, sometimes for the use of archers.
Enceinte	The area enclosed by the castle walls.
Great tower	See **Donjon**.
Groined vault	A cross-vault whose edges are sharply defined.
Hourding	See **Brattice**.
Jamb	The side of an opening through a wall.
Joggled	Keyed together by overlapping joints.
Keep	A word used in England from the 16th century to describe a donjon.

Loop	A narrow opening in a wall that splays out internally, designed either to admit light or for shooting through.
Machicolation	Battlement brought forward on corbels to allow soldiers to command the base of a wall.
Mangonel	Variously used to describe a torsion catapult utilizing a skein of cord as a spring, or a trebuchet, often the type utilizing manpower.
Merlon	The solid section of a battlement.
Mine	A tunnel dug under a wall to weaken the foundations and bring it down.
Moat	A ditch, either wet or dry.
Motte	An earth mound.
Mural chamber	A vaulted chamber formed in the thickness of a wall.
Mural passage	A vaulted passage formed in the thickness of a wall.
Mural tower	A tower set along a curtain wall.
Murder hole	A hole in a passage vault or ceiling through which offensive material could be dropped on attackers, or water to douse fires.
Parados	A low, inner wall of a wall walk.
Parapet	The outer wall of a wall walk.
Petrary	A stone-throwing catapult.
Pilaster	A shallow pier built against a wall to buttress it.
Portcullis	A lattice made from wood clad in iron, or occasionally in iron alone, dropped to block a gate.
Postern	A small rear door.
Putlog	A hole in a wall designed to take the beams that support scaffolding.
Rampart	An earthen bank.
Revetment	The side of a ditch, bank or motte faced with wood, stone or brick.
Ring-work	A circular or oval earthwork with bank and ditch.
Scarp	The side of a ditch.
Spur	A solid, pointed stone reinforcement at the base of a tower; also, a finger of high ground.
Trebuchet	A catapult whose throwing arm utilizes the principle of counterbalance.
Truss	A timber frame designed to support a roof.
Turning bridge	A bridge like a see-saw, the rear half falling into a pit as the front section is raised.
Turret	A small tower.
Vault	A curved ceiling of stone.
Vice	A spiral stair.
Wall walk	A passage along the top of a wall.
Ward	See **Bailey**.
Wattle	Stakes interwoven with branches, used for walling.

INDEX